Telecommute!

Other Books by Lisa Shaw

Time Off From Work

The 100 Best Retirement Businesses (Upstart)

The Upstart Guide to Owning & Managing a
Bed & Breakfast (Upstart)

The Upstart Guide to Owning & Managing an
Antiques Business (Upstart)

The Upstart Guide to Owning & Managing a
Newsletter Business (Upstart)

The Under-35 Guide to Starting & Running
Your Own Business (Upstart/Dearborn)

Published by Lisa Shaw

Travel Marketing Bulletin

The Business Traveler's Guide to Inns and B&Bs

Sticks

Telecommute!

Go to Work without Leaving Home

LISA SHAW

JOHN WILEY & SONS, INC.

New York • Chichester • Brisbane • Toronto • Singapore

For Agnes,
the best telecommuter around

This text is printed on acid-free paper.

Copyright © 1996 by Lisa Shaw
Published by John Wiley & Sons, Inc.

This publication is designed to provide accurate and authoritative
information in regard to the subject matter covered. It is sold with
the understanding that the publisher is not engaged in rendering
legal, accounting, or other professional services. If legal advice or
other expert assistance is required, the services of a competent professional person should be sought.

Library of Congress Cataloging-in-Publication Data

Shaw, Lisa Angowski Rogak.
    Telecommute! : go to work without leaving home / Lisa Shaw.
        p.   cm.
    Includes index.
    ISBN 0-471-11820-6 (pbk. : alk. paper)
    1. Telecommuting—United States.   I. Title.
HD2336.35.U6S53   1996
331.25—dc20   96-1326

Printed in the United States of America
10 9 8 7 6 5 4 3 2 1

Contents

Contents

Introduction

When I first started writing for a living, I used a trusty IBM Selectric typewriter—remember them?—the same kind that I learned to type on when I was a kid. When I used it to write magazine articles in the early to mid-1980s, the idea of using a computer to write was just starting to get some ink in the national media. But having suffered through a primitive programming course in high school and witnessing what a friend had to go through to organize his files on his computer—it took about ten hours to set it all up, which seemed to me a colossal waste of time—I consigned myself to being one of the technologically impaired.

Then the Macintosh came along. I watched as a boss primarily checked his bank balances with it and used it as a Rolodex. Again, it seemed like a waste of time as well as an expensive toy.

Then I had to write a 6,000-word magazine article that went through about six drafts. As my wrists began to tingle, I thought, there must be a better way.

The same thought has undoubtedly crossed your mind about your job as you sit endlessly in rush-hour traffic, buy your seventh pair of pantyhose of the week—and it's only Tuesday—or are confronted with the office grump the minute you step off the elevator. You like your job, but you hate everything that you have to go through in order to do it properly. A light bulb may have appeared over your head at these times: Why can't I just work at home and save myself the aggravation?

The truth is that you probably can. Like the computers that facilitate telecommuting for many employees, flexible work arrangements began to catch on in the 1980s as more people began to see that there was more to life than working eighty hours a week.

In the 1970s women entered the American corporate work force in record numbers. In the 1980s they began to demand flexible work arrangements to meet their personal needs, which often included child care.

In the 1990s, technology has enabled millions of employees—both men and women—to work out of their homes for their companies for at least part of the workweek. With a computer, phone, and fax machine, it's almost as if the employee is in the next cubicle, not several towns—or states—away.

Corporations are more receptive to telecommuting in part because it helps to cut down on the amount of office space needed. And as more states enact trip-reduction laws specifically aimed at large corporations, more companies are going to be required to tell an increasing number of employees to work at home.

In a sense, even though I am self-employed, I've always been a telecommuter. I work out of my home, and different companies send me work through the mail, over the fax, and on the phone. One of my specialties is consulting with people who want to move to the country. Their biggest concern is that they can't find a good job in the rural area to which they want to move. Then I mention telecommuting to them, and their eyes light up.

If you're thinking about moving three hours away from your company, you'll probably want to work at home more than one day out of the week. But I've heard lots of horror stories about people who move to rural developments in places like eastern Pennsylvania and then spend three hours each way commuting to and from their jobs in Manhattan. Every day! What a waste. As someone who's always worked from home, I'd rather try hard drugs or poverty first.

By its very nature, telecommuting appeals to people who want to work at home but who don't necessarily want to start a business. They want to start living their own lives, but they don't want to give up all of their security—yet. Sometimes telecommuters are able to see the independence they get from calling their own shots, and a few years later they are confident enough in their abilities to start their own businesses. Many become independent consultants working for their previous company.

But this is jumping the gun. Although some people welcome the chance to work at home, many will view the opportunity with apprehension. Telecommuting will work for you if you are self-motivated, you work for a company that is not stuck in the mud when it comes to employee options, and/or you want to move to a rural area but would like to hold onto your current job in the city.

With this arrangement, unless your main duty is data entry, you'll probably have to live within a few hours of the office to maintain a satisfactory working relationship. Many telecommuters will still need to check in with the office at least half a day each week, and most feel less isolated if they're able to do so. However, I have heard of an attorney who moved from Chicago to Vermont and is still considered a full employee at the firm. She does fly back once a month to spend several days with her associates, bringing them up to date on her progress and vice versa. Her primary function is legal research, so armed with a fax machine, computer, and telephone, she can feasibly perform this work anywhere she wants—all with the blessing of the law firm.

Telecommuting works most often when you are already working for a company. If you were to move to a rural area and then approach a company in the area about a job in which you could work at home, the chances are that you'd be turned down flat. At the very least, they'd want to try you out in-house first to see if you're a good employee and to get a sense of your strengths and weaknesses. So the person most likely to agree to a telecommuting arrangement is your present boss.

The benefit of telecommuting most often cited is an increase in productivity. Just think—no more wasted meetings or hours spent listening to the office drone who just won't take the hint and leave you alone. No more ringing phones breaking your concentration, unless you plan to spend a good part of your workday at home on the phone anyway. If you don't necessarily have to work from 9 to 5 and your home situation allows for it, you can work at the times of day when you work best and are most productive.

The first thing you should do is make sure you're cut out for telecommuting—not everybody is. Before you move, try working from home a couple of days each week. Over the course of several months, you can then make the transition to full-time telecommuting.

Telecommuting is beginning to shape up as one of the major changes to affect the American workplace in the 1990s. As such, employees are going to find that their employers, increasingly, are on their side.

1

Why Telecommuting Now?

These days trends seem to come from out of nowhere and garner a lot of press overnight. All eyes turn toward whatever happens to be hot at the moment, from new concepts in the business world to expensive sports cars that look like throat lozenges. Such fads are usually very popular for awhile and then either fade into the background as consumers become blasé about them or disappear entirely as their primary appeal wears off.

On the surface, that's how it would appear to be with telecommuting, in which an employee works most often at home or in a branch office away from the corporate headquarters. "Yeah," you may think, "it's great to work at home and still pull in a paycheck, but you just wait and see, it'll never catch on." Such perceptions are understandable but probably inaccurate. Though telecommuting in any form is a radical departure from the traditional corporate structure Americans has slavishly followed for the last 100 years—work in an office, relax at home—all the signs suggest that this flexible work option will catch on permanently.

What Is Telecommuting?

Many people define a telecommuter as anyone who works outside of a traditional office, whether at home, in a satellite office, or even out of a car. Sometimes a telecommuter will refer to his or her work environment as a "virtual office," generally recognized as a nontraditional space from which one telecommutes. The Midwest Institute for Telecommuting Education, a group that consults with businesses by conducting feasibility studies and implementation seminars, defines telecommuting as the following:

> *Telecommuting is an off-site work arrangement that permits employees to work in or near their homes for all or part of the work week. Thus they "commute" to work by telephone and other telecommunications equipment rather than by car or transit.*

Some people still regard telecommuting as a radical concept. But the U.S. economy is converting from a manufacturing base to an information-based one. Workers who process information tend to work by themselves a good part of the time anyway, which is a prime indication that telecommuting may be here to stay. The equipment necessary to telecommute on a regular basis has been coming down steadily in price, enabling more employees and businesses to pursue the advantages of telecommuting. This increase in technology also means that fewer traditional manufacturing jobs are available, and displaced employees must look for jobs that involve processing information. Link Resources, a New York consulting firm, reports that approximately 58 percent of the U.S. work force had information-based jobs in 1990, and the company predicts that a whopping 70 percent of workers in the United States will be solely employed in the processing of information by 2030.

Three Types of Telecommuting

Though telecommuting commonly refers to working from home, there are actually a couple of variations on this theme:

1. *Working from home.* In this situation employees work from a home office that may contain the same kind of equipment they use back in the central office. However, they may not need such equipment at all if they use telecommuting days to catch up on reading and research or to make phone calls.

2. *Working from a telework center.* Telework centers are typically satellite offices located some distance from the company's main office. These may be used by employees who live nearby and don't want to commute to the main office. The company may also lease part of the space to other companies that have employees who live in the area. Telework centers have an advantage over home offices in that technology and computer equipment can be shared rather than purchased separately for each telecommuter. This makes economic sense for the company, which ends up buying less equipment and using it more efficiently. Telecommuting employees work a couple of days a week from the telework center on a rotating basis, ensuring that computer terminals and workstations are in constant use. By contrast, equipment in home offices lies dormant when the telecommuter comes to work at the main office.

In some cases, companies that opt for telework centers don't have to lease space at all; they may rent space for telecommuting employees as needed. The vendor in the forefront of this trend, Kinko's, offers copying services, computer rental, conference facilities, fax machines, and other office equipment, all on an as-needed basis, which is attractive to smaller companies.

3. *Hoteling.* This form of telecommuting is used most often by sales staff who don't need a fixed desk in an office, but must land somewhere once a week or so to pick up mail, plug into the company's main database, or meet a client. It doesn't really matter which office a hoteling employee lands in; he or she may check in at an office in the southern end of the district one week, typically using a vacant desk or conference room for a couple of hours, and telecommute from the northern part of the region the next week.

These three kinds of telecommuting are defined by location. Two other kinds of telecommuting are defined by structure. One kind is conducted under a formal in-house corporate policy; another, more common kind develops in response to individual employee needs. These informal types of telecommuting are often temporary arrangements agreed upon by both employee and supervisor.

Jack Nilles, known as the father of telecommuting, is credited with coining the term back in 1973. Today he runs a consulting firm, JALA Associates, and he refers to telecommuting as a form of telework, which he defines as work conducted via telecommunications instead of in person. In an article he contributed to the journal *Transportation Research*, Nilles broadens his definition even more:

> *Telecommuting is not a technology or collection of technologies. Rather, it is a work option that reduces dependency on transportation by increasing dependency on information technologies. Telecommuting can be accomplished with no more exotic a technology than a telephone (*Transportation Research 22A, no. 4, (1988): 301–317).

Telecommuting—also commonly referred to as *flexiplace* —applies to everyone from an employee who occasionally works at home during busy periods to minimize interruptions, to a person who regularly spends certain days of the week working from home. The full-time telecommuter is rare; most people say they need to have contact with other people and check in at the office at least once a week. Some small businesses, however, take it to the extreme, with the boss and all the employees working out of their homes. They may get together once a week just to touch base. Such contact in this kind of company often is social and informal.

With telecommuting, the home becomes only one of several work sites employees can choose. Telecommuters can also use satellite offices if the corporation is large enough to have a number of them. Some telecommuting is not voluntary in companies that need to cut costs. For example, IBM recently started closing down leased and owned space and ordering some employees to work from home. By cutting out leased space, companies can transfer real estate costs to their employees. Right now the idea works because many employees are dying to work at home. But the balance could be tipped if some employees don't have households where it's possible to work or don't do well working alone.

Telecommuting: A Growing Trend

Telecommuting is catching on across the country for a number of reasons.

Futurist Alvin Toffler, author of *Future Shock* and *The Third Wave*, frequently foretold that millions of U.S. workers would work at home in what he dubbed "electronic cottages." He also predicted that massive urban office buildings would stand empty, but this hasn't come to pass—yet.

One surprising ally of telecommuting is the current Speaker of the House, Newt Gingrich. In a panel discussion on National Public Radio about the future direction of the United States, Gingrich cited Toffler's model of transforming society from a second-wave mechanical bureaucratic society to a third-wave information society. "If we're really serious about distance medicine, distance learning, and distance work," he told NPR's Margot Adler, "we could revolutionize the quality of life in rural America, creating the greatest explosion of new opportunity for rural America in history. Yet we currently are moving in the opposite direction, so that at a time when the IRS should be making it easier to have a home office, they make it harder."

Gingrich is talking about overturning what is known as the Soliman decision, which places stringent restrictions on how a home-office tax deduction can be taken. The Contract with America hints at such reform, and Gingrich specifically says he wants to relieve at least part of the tax burden placed on people who work at home, whether they're entrepreneurs or telecommuters.

Long commutes consume time and energy, make people less productive not only at work but at home, too. Additional time is usually required each day and on the weekend to decompress from the stresses of the week. Telecommuting eliminates some if not all of the stress.

Gingrich and others think telecommuting will grow in popularity for these additional reasons:

□ Rural residents are telecommuting because they need more money than they could otherwise earn in their relatively isolated area. By working for a company that pays more because it is located in an urban area, people not only can earn a decent living but also may stimulate the economy in traditionally depressed regions.

□ People desire to pursue other interests—hobbies, part-time and/or seasonal businesses, even education. Telecommuting saves hours in their day by eliminating travel to work. The extra time can be spent on these outside pursuits.

□ Telecommuters save money because they're not spending it on lunches out, tolls, gas, parking, and clothes for work.

When Jack Nilles coined the word "telecommuting" back in 1973, the practice was promoted as a way to deal with the energy shortage of the 1970s. Now companies are under federal mandate (as specified in the Clean Air Act) to do their part to reduce air pollution by drawing up trip-reduction strategies. The law is already in effect in California, New York, and New Jersey. Generally, there are five ways to reduce commuting: subsidized bus passes, ride sharing, flex time, van pooling, and telecommuting.

In addition, the Americans with Disabilities Act (ADA) requires businesses of a certain size to employ a certain percentage of people who are disabled, whether they are legally blind or wheelchair-bound. Instead of going through the time and hassle of arranging for private transportation or dealing with the aggravation of public transportation, both companies and employees alike prefer setting the employee up in a home office. And rather than physically remodeling public and private buildings—widening doorways and entrances, altering restrooms, building wheelchair ramps, readjusting elevator buttons—for disabled Americans, more employers are looking to telecommuting.

Why Are People More Interested in Telecommuting?

When asked if they would like to start working from home, even a day or two a week, many people automatically respond, "Sure." Their minds start racing with thoughts of all the things they'd do if they could use commuting time for personal or family matters instead. Frequently, however, they cut themselves short by thinking of all of the reasons why they can't telecommute or why their bosses won't let them.

The fact is that more people—employees and employers alike—are thinking about telecommuting, and here's why:

☐ *The need for a balanced life.* People have recently begun to see that work isn't everything. They want to better integrate their working and personal lives, and telecommuting is one way to free up more time for themselves.

☐ *The desire to accomplish what you want for a change.* Several generations of Americans have been unfairly branded as selfish. The truth is that many people—especially women —are more selfless than the media makes them out to be. Here, too, people seek balance: In order to give to others, one has to give to oneself as well. And working from home is a great way to start.

☐ *The desire to break through the glass ceiling or rise above the sticky floor.* If you haven't already made it to where you thought you should have been by now, then your chances of ever reaching the upper echelons of your company or industry probably aren't good—unless you start doing things differently. Freeing up more time in your day by eliminating a long commute can help you get the most out of your career.

☐ *The desire to explore a particular interest.* When you're young and idealistic, it's easy to envision reaching your career goals by the age of twenty-five. In most cases, of course, real life intercedes, and the need to make a living pushes your main focus to the back burner, where it remains until retirement, if it manages to resurface at all. But sometimes, everyday life—the job, the family, the bills—just becomes too much to bear, and you figure,

"Dammit, I work hard, why shouldn't I be able to do what I want?" By working from home you'll not only have more free time but also drastically reduce your stress levels. And you'll save money on transportation, lunches out, and office clothes, among other things, allowing you to spend more freely on a special interest.

☐ *Refusal to buy into the corporate structure.* Millions of baby boomers poured into the mainstream labor markets in the 1970s and 1980s. Some immediately saw all the warts and left; most decided to stick it out. But when things didn't get much better, they decided to take matters into their own hands by working out of their homes, where they could get their work done in peace and quiet and avoid the constant onslaught of office politics that seems to consume so much of an employee's day.

No doubt at least one of your reasons for wanting to telecommute is listed above. Some of you might agree with every item on the list, yet remain convinced that the best thing to do is to suffer in silence—you need your job, you don't want to jeopardize your boss's opinion of you, the economy's tight, and . . . .

Don't think like this. Once you declare your intention to start working from home, most of the negative reaction you'll receive will come from coworkers who see your desire to telecommute as disturbing the status quo. "What makes you think you're better than the rest of us?" colleagues might ask—that is, if they even have the guts to bring it up with you. "Why do you think you have what it takes to get what you want if the rest of us can't?"

But you're not just like the rest; you're taking steps to live the kind of life that suits you. Read on how to find out how others have dealt with people who wanted to see them fail and what standing up for yourself will ultimately mean to your life.

Who's Telecommuting?

Men and women from large and small companies all over the United States are telecommuting because they want to achieve more balance in their lives. Though experts warn that working from home does not necessarily allow parents to take care of their preschoolers, many fathers and mothers of young children do choose to telecommute so they can spend more time with their families. They can still spend a good deal of time with their kids in the daytime by breaking up their job duties into manageable two- and three-hour chunks.

People who live in rural areas but work for urban employers are choosing to telecommute so they can enjoy a country lifestyle yet still pull in a city income. Others choose to telecommute because interruptions keep them from getting much done during office hours, so they end up bringing their work home at night. If they were telecommuting, they'd probably be able to get all of their work done during the daytime, leaving the evening hours free.

Employees who must spend most of their working time out on the road often give their company a competitive edge. Most of these workers are sales reps who travel to visit clients, either locally or in more far-flung locales. If they're able to hook into their company's mainframe while they're out there, they can receive all kinds of support and further sharpen that competitive edge, which creates more business for their companies.

Another factor in the rise of telecommuting is the increased role of women in the work force in the last few decades. Whether they telecommute in order to take care of a child, cut commute time, or simply balance their home and work lives more evenly, the fact is that women have been the prime movers in creating flexible job situations, from job sharing to flex time. However, it shouldn't be argued that telecommuting is better for women than men or that women are its primary beneficiaries. According to Arlene A. Johnson, vice president at the Families and Work Institute in New York, more telecommuters are male than female. In fact, in an article on telecommuting for *PC World* (October 1994), Johnson claimed that telecommuting is the single flexible work arrangement that hasn't been "feminized," or seen by managers and companies as a concession that affects mostly women. It may have avoided this label because the earliest telecommuters in the late 1970s and 1980s were computer programmers and technical-support analysts, who were overwhelmingly male. Though it may seem that women benefit most from telecommuting, and are flocking to it in droves, the truth is that men choose telecommuting for the same reasons that women do.

It has been difficult to estimate how many telecommuters there are in the United States, because the definition of telecommuting is frequently muddled. Some studies lump people who work at home for an employer together with self-employed men and women who work out of a home office. Some companies have informal policies on telecommuting and others have guerrilla telecommuters, whose work arrangement may be unknown even to the person in the next office.

The best estimate is that 6.1 percent of American workers telecommute at least part-time. According to Link's 1993 National Work-at-Home Survey, about 7.6 million people (4.1 million men and 3.5 million women) work at home at least part of the time, up from 6.6 million just one year earlier. In 1995, almost 9 million American employees telecommuted at least one day a week.

Even celebrities are getting into the act of telecommuting. Special fiber-optic lines, which are capable of transmitting complex music, documents, and images, are now being used in Hollywood and New York studios to dub in dialogue after a movie is made, record duets being sung simultaneously from different continents, and create sound mixes so seamless that you would never be able to tell the singer was on one coast while the musicians were on another.

A company named Entertainment Digital Network (EDnet) provides producers and engineers in the entertainment industry with the ability to transmit and receive audio and video through compressed digital messages. In 1994 celebrity telecommuters included Ben Kingsley, who used the service to redub several lines for the movie *Searching for Bobby Fischer*, and Frank Sinatra, who sang his half of a duet from Los Angeles while his partner, Liza Minelli, was in Brazil. As singers and actors increasingly move away from the bustle of New York and Los Angeles to Montana, Connecticut, and even Europe, EDnet will make it more possible for the stars to telecommute.

Many telecommuters work for small businesses that have no formal telecommuting policy; others have jumped through a few hoops in order to meet the restrictions of a Fortune 500 company, where presence is largely still considered the best indicator of productivity and company loyalty. There may be employees at your company who are telecommuting without your knowing it; they may be sales reps who live and work out of their cars, or they may have an agreement with their supervisors to work at home whenever the amount of work that requires concentration and quiet time exceeds one day's worth. There's a good chance that several of the people you spoke with today—at home or at the office—were working from the comfort of their own homes. This is the ideal in telecommuting—to integrate home and office so seamlessly that customers and clients never suspect that the person on the other end of the phone or computer is actually a telecommuter.

Studies report that the traditional forty-hour work

schedule creates some kind of hardship for approximately 33 percent of all American workers, be it dealing with child care and school vacations or spending more money on a reliable car in which to commute. In families with tightly packed schedules, one mishap can bring down the whole teetering infrastructure. Most families know this, which causes a lot of the stress inherent in the two-working-parent families that are common today.

According to Pacific Bell, after the Northridge earthquake in January 1994, many people began telecommuting temporarily to avoid commutes that could last four hours one way. A good number were still telecommuting a year later, long after the freeways were fully repaired. In fact, nine of every ten "earthquake telecommuters" were still working from home at least part-time a year later. Susan Herman of the City of Los Angeles's Department of Telecommunications says telecommuting has definitely eased the flow of rush-hour commuter traffic in the city. "The kind of traffic congestion that you normally experience has been reduced," she told syndicated columnist Michael Schrage, who regularly tracks how technology is affecting personal and professional life. "Travel is minutes quicker. It's like losing weight: it takes time to be perceptible, but it's definitely there."

Telecommuting Snapshot

Among telecommuters in 1992, 32 percent worked less than eight hours from home each week, 51 percent telecommuted between eight and thirty-four hours a week, and only 17 percent worked thirty-five or more hours in a week from home.

Reasons Telecommuting Will Continue to Grow

All current societal signs suggest that telecommuting will become more popular in the next five years. In fact, according to the Gartner Group, a consulting firm in Stamford, Connecticut, that regularly reports on telecommuting, 80 percent of U.S. companies will have at least 30 percent of their employees working outside of the traditional workplace, whether at home, in a telework center, or in a mobile office, by the year 2000. Let's take a look at the reasons why.

☐ *Traffic.* Traffic congestion creates so much stress for workers, even those taking public transportation, that more and more Americans will look for other employment options, whether that means taking a lower-paying job closer to home, quitting their jobs to stay at home with the kids, or telecommuting part- or full-time.

☐ *Generation X.* As the baby-boom generation moves up through the ranks and into early retirement, there are fewer entry-level employees around to replace them, simply because there were fewer babies born into the generation that followed, which has been disparagingly tagged "Generation X." The labor pool of employees with specific talents will be smaller, so employers will be more willing to make concessions in order to hold onto their valued employees. In addition, members of this generation are just beginning to start having families, and they, unlike their fathers, the "gray flannel suits" of the 1950s and 1960s, appear determined to spend time with their kids and spouses.

☐ *Technology.* Perhaps the biggest reason telecommuting is starting to become a more viable option for millions of American workers is the advent of affordable high-tech computers and other office equipment, which make it easy for an employee to work anywhere and still be connected to the office.

The History of Telecommuting

Gil Gordon, a telecommuting consultant who publishes a monthly newsletter called *Telecommuting Review,* has seen telecommuting grow from something that both companies and employees laughed at to a viable corporate work style in which everyone benefits. He got his first glimpse of what telecommuting could mean for U.S. business in 1981. Gordon had been working in human resources for ten years and was looking to strike out on his own. He attended a conference of human resource people in 1981 and was struck by one of the speakers' remarks about the coming demographic changes in the workplace. "He talked about an increase of women in the work force, while somebody in the audience quoted a *New York Times* story about Alvin Toffler's then-new book, *The Third Wave,* that described something called the electronic cottage," says Gordon. "Someone asked the speaker what he thought of these trends, and he said that except for a few oddballs and hermits, nobody would be interested in working from home."

Gordon, struck by how quickly the speaker dismissed the idea, did some research. He found that people and companies were embracing telecommuting for the wrong reasons. The idea was driven by employees in high-tech jobs who tended to be concerned only with technology issues. That was just the spur Gordon needed. At the time the IBM PC had just been released, and the era of personal computing was just beginning. In addition, commuting and traffic problems were just starting to show up outside of the main cities, and corporations had begun to move out of the middle of cities and into the suburbs, which laid the groundwork for the ninety-minute commutes so common today. "Although it was really a shot in the dark, trying to get corporations to see the value of telecommuting, it did seem to make sense to me, since I saw that many people could benefit from it as well as their companies," says Gordon. Indeed, telecommuting was an idea whose time had come, and Gordon doesn't think that it could have happened much earlier. "Some people had written about telecommuting in the mid-1970s," he says, "but the lack of computer portability got in the way."

Joanne Pratt, a telecommuting consultant, has been involved in the field since 1980. She says the people who were telecommuting when she first got started were pioneers, and it cost a lot less money for a company to set up an employee to work at home than in an office. "They simply didn't have the tools," says Pratt. "The type of job that was most amenable for an employee to work at home tended to be data entry."

Beginning in the mid-1980s, however, many American workers started to evaluate the lack of balance between their personal and professional lives. The work-'til-you-drop, go-go pace of the 1980s helped cause this widespread reevaluation, and people began to search for a way to get their work done yet still enjoy their home lives.

As a result, employees began to see the value of working at home at least a couple of days a week. With any innovation , there's always going to be a small group of people who eagerly adopt the change, a larger group of people who follow suit, and finally, the largest group—people who jump in the water when everything else is safe. Gordon believes that in the mid-1990s telecommuting finds itself between the second and third stages. Telecommuting has been shown to be workable; it's no longer perceived as experimental or risky. You have to work hard to mess it up. Some companies, however, ignore the accumulated data about what it takes to do it well. That's a mistake, because not everyone is well suited to telecommuting.

The idea of telecommuting is not new. It's been used in primitive form for years by traveling salesmen and customer service representatives who visit clients at their place of business. What's changed is that telecommuting has been adapted for many different types of jobs that had previously kept workers moored in an office somewhere. Computers and other technological advances are largely responsible for the expansion of the definition of telecommuting.

The Benefits to the Employee

Clearly, as you'll see in chapter 2, companies that implement telecommuting programs receive specific benefits, both financial and corporate. Here are the advantages that their employees enjoy:

☐ Less commuting time, more time for other things

☐ Job stability: It's less likely that an employee will search for another job with another company, since the current job can be performed anywhere.

☐ More time for family

☐ More time for leisure pursuits

☐ Less stress, better health

☐ Less money spent on gas, clothes, and meals out

Frank Damico of Bell Atlantic, who both telecommutes and supervises other telecommuters at the company, says telecommuting has helped him become more organized in both his personal and professional lives. "With telecommuting, most of our communication is in writing," he says. "Dealing face-to-face with other workers in the office, most of the communication is verbal. I've seen that telecommuting has almost forced us to make better use of our time."

Damico adds that, for him, the ultimate value of

telecommuting has been its flexibility. "There's absolutely no reason why a person can't work at home two days this week, four days the next week, and zero days the following week," he says. Damico prefers that telecommuting be used in this way to help meet deadlines, work within quotas, and deal with downtime. He rejects the cookie-cutter mentality that says a person must work at home the same days each week.

The statistics on gas savings alone are mind-boggling. If 20,000 employees who regularly commute ten miles each way choose instead to work at home three days a week, more than 12.5 million gallons of gasoline will be saved in the course of one year. As President Bush pointed out to the California Chamber of Commerce at a 1991 conference on federal air-pollution mandates, "A typical 20-minute round-trip commute to work over the course of a year adds up to two very stressful 40-hour weeks lost on the road. If only 5 percent of the commuters in Los Angeles County telecommuted one day each week, they'd save 205 million miles of travel each year and keep 47,000 tons of pollutants from entering the atmosphere. So telecommuting means saving energy, improving air quality, and quality of life. Not a bad deal."

The Downside of Telecommuting

Of course, telecommuting does have its downside, and it's not for everyone. Even the happiest of telecommuters I interviewed admitted to some disadvantages of working from home:

- ☐ You may feel isolated without the regular social contact of the office.

- ☐ You may find it difficult to motivate yourself.

- ☐ You may find that it's hard to stop working at the end of the day.

- ☐ Your neighbors may drop in to socialize, and you may find it hard to turn them away.

- ☐ It may be hard to resist the refrigerator, TV, or other distractions in your home.

The biggest obstacles for both employees and employers to telecommuting include the following:

- ☐ Management doesn't believe in supervising in absentia.

- ☐ Telecommuters are less able to meet the needs of customers.

- ☐ Teams break down when members are scattered.

- ☐ Telecommuting favors some employees over others.

- ☐ Meetings must be planned in advance.

- ☐ Future promotions may be affected.

- ☐ Managers must spend more time supervising and use different methods.

As with anything that's useful to some part of the population, there are people who denigrate the possibilities of telecommuting. Steve G. Steinberg writes in the May 1994 issue of *Wired* that the majority of employees in the United States believe it's necessary to have a presence in the office in order to be fairly considered for promotions. This perception, which Steinberg believes will impede the growth of telecommuting, is off the mark. As managers are increasingly educated about the increased productivity of their telecommuting employees, attitudes will change. Indeed, many of the telecommuters interviewed in this book were promoted despite working from home; in fact, telecommuting may even have facilitated their promotions.

The Best Jobs for Telecommuting

It seems that some jobs were made for telecommuting. They demand peace and quiet, a minimum of interruptions, and concentration. If your job is on the following list, telecommuting may make it easier for you to work, but it doesn't mean you're off the hook when it comes to other aspects of your job, such as meeting quotas or deadlines you set up with your employer.

According to a study conducted by JALA Associates, about half of all employees could do their jobs just as well from home or a telework center as from the main corporate headquarters. In addition, almost a third could easily fulfill about half of their job responsibilities by working from home. Only about one-third hold jobs for which it would be extremely difficult to justify telecommuting.

Here are some ideal jobs for telecommuters:

- Writer/reporter/book editor
- Data-entry clerk
- Computer programmer
- Engineer
- Sales representative
- Secretary or administrative assistant
- Insurance agent
- Marketing manager
- Bookkeeper
- Translator
- Stockbroker

The Worst Jobs for Telecommuting

If you see your job on the following list, don't despair—you may still be able to telecommute in one form or another.

It's highly unlikely, however, that you'll be able to telecommute full-time with one of these jobs. Rather, you may be able to do some of your work at home, perhaps the kind of tasks that involve entering data, writing reports, or reading technical journals.

- ☐ Managers who work at high levels within a company
- ☐ Employees at lower levels who need feedback and constant supervision
- ☐ Service workers (how can a retail salesperson telecommute?)
- ☐ Manufacturing workers (how can you work on the line from home?)
- ☐ Health care professionals (employees have to go to where their patients are)

Telecommuting Snapshot

Here are some other statistics about telecommuting, as compiled by the Gartner Group, a consulting firm in Stamford, Connecticut, that regularly conducts studies on the subject:

- ☐ The average increase in productivity per telecommuter ranges from 10 percent to 16 percent.
- ☐ The amount of money a company saves on office rent and other expenses per year: $3,000 to $5,000.
- ☐ The average telecommuter works in the office only one day out of five.
- ☐ The average telecommuter works two hours more each day than an in-office counterpart.

(continued)

(continued)

☐ The average cost of training and adaption per telecommuter: $1,000 to $1,500.

☐ Companies typically supply each telecommuter with a 486 PC, fax/modem, phone line, printer, some office furniture, and a telephone, at an average cost of $2,000 to $4,000.

PROFILE OF A TELECOMMUTER: FRAN GOLDEN

Fran Golden is the hotel editor and New England bureau chief for *Travel Weekly*, a trade publication for travel agents. She runs her bureau out of a spare bedroom that she's converted into her office in her Swampscott, Massachusetts, home.

She began working for the New Jersey-based magazine in 1984 as a freelancer, moving into a full-time freelance position and then a staff position. Golden had no desire either to move to New Jersey or to work from an office, and she explained that she could handle the work from her home. In 1984, she had also just given birth to her first child and wanted to be able to care for the baby.

The company agreed. Its managers wanted someone in Boston, and the fact that Golden lived in the area allowed the magazine to offer coverage of the New England area. Golden began to work full time. At first the job wasn't much different from what she had done as a freelancer. She wrote her stories and faxed them in from a local copy shop. A few years later, the company upgraded her equipment to include a fax/modem, a PC, and a laser printer. For several years Golden worked from her dining room table, but when she moved to a new house she gained a separate office to which she can close the door. She gave birth to another child in 1987.

Her daily schedule is to get her kids to school around

8 A.M., then take a walk with her dog on the beach. She comes home and works until her kids get out of school at 2:30. What she does after that depends upon the circumstances and whether she has any deadlines. "I might make phone calls and read mail," she says, "but I don't like to write in the late afternoon. I do most of my busy work when my kids are in school."

Actually, Golden started a trend toward telecommuting at the magazine. She was one of the first to start working from home at *Travel Weekly*, but after she started, the magazine added two full-time editors in San Francisco. Then an editor moved to the south shore of Boston from New Jersey. "Finally, the executive editor joked that he'd like to live in Burlington, Vermont, but at that point the boss said no more," said Golden. The paper also has editors working from their homes in Hawaii, Mexico, and Orlando, Florida.

She admits that telecommuting has its disadvantages but says they fall pretty low on the priority scale. "Sometimes I miss being a participant in office politics, because it sometimes seems like I hear everything second and thirdhand," Golden said. For this reason she feels it's important to maintain regular phone contact with other people at the office, especially because she works for a news publication, where so much—stories, research, and leads—relies on the rumors that fly. "Sometimes I feel a little out of it, like they're talking about something involving them instead of me," she says. But in her mind the advantages definitely outweigh the disadvantages.

One of the main reasons Golden chose to work from home was so she could raise her kids. Unlike many telecommuting parents, she has never tried to hide them from people on the phone. "There used to be a joke at the paper about the fact that my kids were always screaming in the background," she laughs. "In fact, some people at the office drew up a Christmas wish list one year, and the wish was that my kids would stop screaming when I was on the phone. It was difficult when I was potty training my kids because you can't tell a kid to wait. I remember I had to put a very senior executive at American Express on hold once and I honestly told him why."

This particular executive took the incident in stride. "I've found that simply because a person I'm interviewing will hear my kids in the background, I seem friendlier and on a more personal basis to a lot of the executives I have to deal with," says Golden. "When I first started to work from home, I would actually nurse my kids when I was doing phone interviews. In fact, it's a great fear of mine that picturephones will actually come to fruition, because right now, for instance, I'm sitting here in shorts. One of the great joys of telecommuting is that I don't have to wash my hair every day or put on nylons. I figure I save $20 a week because I don't have to wear pantyhose."

When Golden first began to telecommute, she dropped by the corporate offices every so often when she traveled to New York City to attend press conferences and other meetings. She doesn't feel obligated anymore. She still tries to have dinner with her boss several times a year when she's in the city but usually doesn't go to the main office. Golden travels a fair amount to do research, and she also tries to set up meetings in Boston. "I do try for that face-to-face contact. There are days when I actually have to get dressed," she jokes.

"I used to feel I had to go down to the corporate offices to ask for a raise, and to attend some of the staff meetings, but members of the staff who telecommute are not required to go," she says. "Besides, a lot of the information in the staff meetings is irrelevant to the bureau anyway."

Many people hesitate to telecommute because they think it will be more difficult to get promoted. Golden has been promoted since she started telecommuting, but she concedes that she really can't go any higher if she continues to work at home. But that's not important to her; being available for her kids is. Now that her kids are older, Golden says, they're involved in more activities and need her to chauffeur them around. "Getting kids to and from after-school activities must be really difficult for people who work from an office," she says. Because she works from home, Golden can do the carpool circuit, and picks her kids up and drops them off at school. "I really like the uninterrupted time and the feeling of independence," she says, adding that she feels more creative in her home environment than she would at a regular office.

When she first started to work at home, Golden had a small problem with friends who would forget she was working and stop by for a chat or for help in "semi-emergencies." Once she set them straight, it ceased to be a problem, although her husband and kids sometimes still interrupt her. Moving into a separate office room where she can close the door has helped alleviate this problem.

Though she can usually get most of her writing work done while her kids are at school, occasionally Golden needs to work at night. She has her kids well trained. "From an early age, my kids knew what 'deadline' meant: 'Mommy's busy, wait'," she says. Another disadvantage of working from home is that it's hard to stop working, says Golden, who completed a book late in 1994 in addition to writing full-time for *Travel Weekly.* "I was in my office a lot, and it was difficult on both me and my family," she says. "It's hard to turn it off. I'll be leaving for a trip and I'll be packing and reading mail and faxes at the same time. And in the middle of the night, if I hear the fax machine go off, I'll want to go read it right then."

Over the years, Golden has come to realize that she can't expect to be at the computer nonstop from 9 to 5. "I always tell people who ask me about telecommuting not to try to work at the computer more than six hours a day. I don't think people in an office realize how much they're interrupted when they're trying to get some work done. If you sit down in front of a computer for six hours, that's a lot of time.

"You have to give yourself breaks once in awhile," she said. "And you have to be realistic about working from home, too. Just because you're home doesn't mean you're going to get your house cleaned. You may find time for some of that, but you shouldn't expect to get a lot of housework done during your workday. I love to cook, and at the end of the day I cook to relax." One advantage of working from home, Golden says, is that she can throw something in the pot and go back to work. She tells other telecommuters that it's not a good idea to stay in the house all the time. "Go out and take a break away from the house," she advises. "Whether it's going to the library or going out for lunch, you don't want to feel isolated."

In 1995, Golden's husband started to work at home, too, as he was taking a sabbatical from his job with the Associated Press. She initially viewed it as somewhat of an invasion but believes it may turn out to be beneficial to the whole family. "I'm into my own little routine—for instance, I'll eat lunch at 10:30 if I want to, or at 1:30—and I expect him to interrupt me while I'm working, at least in the beginning. But if the kids need to be picked up and I'm doing an interview, he could be real helpful."

In the end, Golden says, a person needs to be very well organized in order to successfully work at home, especially full-time. "My office is a series of piles, but they're organized piles, and you also have to be self-motivated because there's nobody looking over your shoulder," she says. "It's important that you're able to go into your office and concentrate and work hard during the hours you've designated. If you're not a self-starter, and if you like to stay in bed until 12, you may not be able to get your job done. And if you're a person who likes a lot of immediate feedback, working at home is not the way to go."

2

Telecommuting and Business

On the whole, American business seems to resist change—unless, that is, some new managerial technique is bandied about as the next best thing. When the next new trend in business rolls down the pike, companies will line up to jump on board.

Now, I'm not saying companies should strive for change for its own sake—indeed, if a business isn't able to stick with one technique or method long enough to see an effect, it can quickly go down the tubes. Both employers and customers will start to view a company like this as a tire-kicker, staying with this year's model only until next year's new one comes along.

Many companies, seem terrified at the prospect of having employees work away from the corporate headquarters, out of the view of the people in charge of supervising them. For large, old corporations in particular, the burgeoning trend of telecommuting may seem like too much to bear. However, younger, smaller, and hungrier businesses commonly view telecommuting as an effective management tool that will put them way ahead of their competition and increase their bottom line. No matter what kind of company you work for, you will be better prepared to approach your boss and ultimately enhance your own telecommuting experience if you understand the concerns businesses have about telecommuting.

You should also be aware that businesses can use telecommuting to take advantage of employment laws. In 1987 men and women who had been telecommuting for Cal Western States Life Insurance Company in Sacramento sued their employer, claiming that Cal Western had abruptly suspended their benefits, including vacation, health insurance, and pension funds. The company asserted that these employees had become independent contractors when they began working at home, but the employees said that they were never informed of the change. Besides, before they began to work for the company out of their homes, all of the telecommuters had been employees of the company and enjoyed full benefits.

In January 1988 Cal Western discontinued its telecommuting program, and a few months later the company settled out of court with the disgruntled employees.

Loyalty in the American Workplace

One factor that has done much to increase the desire to telecommute is the decline in loyalty in the corporate workplace in the last decade. Employees rarely stay with the same company from the minute they get out of school until they reach retirement age; certainly, given the ruthless climate of downsizing going on at many U.S. corporations, many of which show record profits even as they distribute pink slips quite freely, most employees have an eye peeled for something better. In this age of disloyalty, telecommuting can encourage employees to stay with their present companies, and managers can use it to entice the more talented and valuable employees in the corporation to stay.

As the U.S. economy's focus continues to shift from manufacturing to information processing, the work force as a whole will continue to become more independent, as working with information requires more self-sufficiency and motivation. Therefore, more employees believe they will succeed at telecommuting.

Telecommuting also reduces absenteeism. A person who works from home probably feels more loyalty toward his or her company for the consideration and convenience than a coworker who must trudge into the office five days a week and isn't happy with the job to begin with. Which employee is more likely to take a sick day at the first sign of the sniffles? The telecommuting employee will be more likely to muddle through a workday at home despite not feeling well, not only because it's more comfortable at home but also because he or she doesn't have to commute to the office. The nontelecommuting employee is more likely to take a sick day to avoid the unpleasant experience of getting dressed and traveling into the office when feeling under the weather.

Companies that encourage employees to telecommute can push the fact that they care about their employees and the environment. In this age where companies have to pay attention to social issues, clean up the earth, and provide their employees with more well-rounded lives, all the while closely watching the bottom line, telecommuting provides an attractive selling point and public relations tool.

Companies in the technology field can use telecommuting to demonstrate that they practice what they preach and that their employees are well-versed in their customers' business problems. For instance, a company that sells modems or communications software can point to its own telecommuting employees as satisfied users of this equipment. They may even go one step further by having these staff members available to provide detailed testimonials whenever a customer has a question about product effectiveness.

Moreover, telecommuting can help companies meet federal and state law requiring them to employ people with disabilities, for whom getting to the office is always a hassle. In fact, many companies have a mission statement that clearly states the goal of hiring more employees with disabilities. However, such workers' transportation needs frequently get in the way. As a result, many companies fall short of their goals in this area.

The Americans with Disabilities Act (ADA) specifies that employers must accommodate a disabled employee in a variety of ways if the employee is able to adequately perform the job. For a deaf person, this might mean that the company must supply a special TTD keyboard allowing the employee to communicate with coworkers as well as with other people over the phone. For employees who might not be able to get around easily, or who perhaps suffer from a debilitating psychological condition such as agoraphobia, telecommuting seems to be a perfect solution.

However, undoubtedly some employers will use telecommuting to segregate disabled people from the rest of the work force. It's ironic, because the ADA is intended to increase access for physically challenged workers, not to decrease it. In fact, if federal investigators discover that a company has been using telecommuting to a fault, then that employer can actually be cited for violating the act, especially if other options to accommodate disabled employees are available.

Why Businesses Like Telecommuting

IBM's new sales office building in Cranford, New Jersey, is as spartan as it gets in this new age of downsizing and reengineering. It's a converted warehouse; no decorator has been here, showing how far the company has come from the days of walnut-paneled offices and astronomical profit margins. There are 220 metal desks scattered throughout the cavernous space, but only about 50 people sit at them. Where are the other sales reps? Out on the road or at their home offices. In fact, the people currently sitting at the desks are merely borrowing them. Each sales rep averages about a day a week in this office, some even less. This warehouse serves as a pit stop where employees can pick up their mail, confer with colleagues, and update the hard drives on their laptop computers with new pricing structures, technical information, and product information. The desks are devoid of both people and equipment: only a chair, a phone, and a computer jack can be found.

When IBM moved its sales force to this windowless warehouse in 1994, the site wasn't the only drastic change. The number of sales reps was literally cut in half, and two levels of management were totally eliminated.

Downsizing is causing companies to take telecommuting seriously, as it allows them to reduce their overhead across the board. Having telecommuters on staff means that less money will be spent on office rent, utilities, and other in-office expenses, and most figures show that an employee's productivity will increase if some of the stress of getting to the office is eliminated and additional time is made available in a worker's day.

In many major cities, office space can be a company's biggest expenditure. Increasingly, businesses are relying on telecommuting to help them cut costs. In 1994 IBM reduced its total office space by 22 million square feet, the equivalent of the space of eight Empire State Buildings. The new converted warehouse in Cranford, New Jersey, is only 400,000 square feet. In the Northeast alone, IBM saved $70 million in real estate expenses in 1994.

IBMers in the Midwest have been affected as well. Of the 4,000 IBM employees scattered throughout the Midwest, fully 2,500 work mostly from their homes, cars, and customers' offices. As in New Jersey, when Midwest IBMers want to come to the office, they must call first to reserve a desk and phone.

This version of telecommuting is frequently referred to as "hoteling"—an employee has to reserve a desk the same way he has to reserve a hotel room. Unlike hotels, however, corporate offices don't offer luxury accommodations; everyone gets the same spartan environment and equipment.

The difference between the way IBM instituted telecommuting and the way most other companies do it is that Big Blue basically told its sales staff it had to fish or cut bait. In other words, do it our way, or don't do it at all. Though some consultants would frown at this nonvoluntary approach, it's clear that other companies still occasionally follow IBM's lead, especially when it comes to massive downsizing strategies. That's bad news for managers who like to reward employees with the chance to spend a day or two a week working from home. They'll have to think up some new rewards.

But IBM's approach wasn't all negative. It turns out that the Midwest bureau needed to cut costs but didn't want to cut staff. Telecommuting enabled it to save jobs. Moreover, with many voluntary telecommuting programs, the employee is responsible for buying his or her own equipment. When a program is mandatory, the company usually supplies and pays for all equipment and peripherals. Therefore, IBM telecommuters did not incur heavy start-up costs.

However, the danger with mandatory programs is that many employees think that being banished from working in the office full-time is the worst kind of punishment they could get.

Currently, 41 percent of all U.S. companies offer telecommuting to all of its employees, according to a 1994 survey by the Conference Board, an organization that monitors U.S. workplace trends. The Conference Board survey showed that of those firms offering telecommuting, 72 percent offer it only to selected employees. Managers and supervisors account for fully half of telecommuters at these surveyed companies. Not surprisingly, only 2 percent of employees who belong to a union reported that they telecommute. Sixty-eight percent of the companies supply their telecommuting employees with equipment such as computers, phones, and office supplies, but not office furniture.

A good harbinger for the future of telecommuting is the fact that even business schools are getting into the act. Purdue University now allows master's students in its business program to spend most of their time working at home while holding down regular jobs. Over the course of a two-year program, students spend six two-week periods on campus. The rest of the time they continue their studies at home, communicating with their professors and fellow students by e-mail, fax, and phone. When they do attend classes, it's not just a short commute for all students, some of whom have flown into the West Lafayette, Indiana, campus from points as diverse as Albuquerque and Puerto Rico.

The University of Pittsburgh offers a similar program, as does Bowling Green State in Ohio; both of these schools grant MBAs. Though these universities have no statistics on how many of their telecommuting students also telecommute at their regular jobs, you can't help but think that once they get this telecommuting experience under their belts, they'll be more likely to want to continue telecommuting and will be better managers of their telecommuting employees.

Not surprisingly, small businesses are helping to lead the telecommuting revolution in the United States. According to Link Resources, businesses that have fewer than 100 employees employ more than 80 percent of the telecommuters nationwide. The reasons? Small businesses are more flexible than larger companies, where the tiniest detail of every new program has to go through a number of committees before it can be instituted. In addition, small companies are more immediately concerned about their bottom lines than are bigger companies, despite all the headlines about massive downsizings by Fortune 500 firms. If a company with 50 employees can save a few thousand dollars a year, it's a big deal, while such amounts are mere pocket change to the name-brand companies.

Telecommuting also allows specialized companies to find employees no matter where they live. For instance, many rural residents could have worked at high-powered, challenging jobs in the city but felt it was more important to live in less hectic surroundings. They just resigned themselves to making less money. Telecommuting has changed all that, allowing such men and women to work for high-paying urban employers. For instance, the Vermont Department of Development and Community Affairs is currently working with the University of Vermont, Vermont Technical College, and NYNEX to allow people who live in the state's Northeast Kingdom—traditionally Vermont's poorest, most unemployment-plagued area—to telecommute from their homes as they work for the state tourism department.

When Bell Atlantic allowed fifty managers to telecommute on a trial basis, more than 27 percent of the participants said their productivity increased, and the other 73 percent worked at the same level of performance. The company projected that over a full year the fifty managers would save $15,000 in gasoline, parking fees, and public transportation costs.

"Currently, the American workplace is going from being a very static, moored work force where everybody's in the same place at the same time to a highly mobile work force that enables companies to operate globally," says telecommuting consultant Joanne Pratt. Over time, companies undoubtedly will start to see the benefits of telecommuting on their bottom line.

Jack Robertson, marketing manager at Pacific Bell, says telecommuting initially was a technical issue at the company, as most of the employees needed to be connected into the corporate databases. However, in the mid-1990s telecommuting at Pacific Bell has turned into more of a cultural and personal attraction. A good percentage of the company's workers have become interested in telecommuting after seeing how it would directly affect their lives. "Today, the main problem is that management prevents more employees from telecommuting, even within Pacific Bell, which is largely a progressive company," says Robertson. "Some managers are still used to managing by walking around, but the culture here and elsewhere is drastically changing, since the issue has become defocused by necessity."

He's referring to the fact that most companies initially explore telecommuting in order to meet Clean Air regulations. Robertson helps outside companies to work with Pacific Bell by setting their employees up to telecommute. "But back about 1993, we stopped promoting telecommuting solely as a way that companies could meet the Clean Air standards because we were seeing that there were more benefits that could be attributed to telecommuting right down to the bottom line. And that began to turn telecommuting into a viable solution for many companies," says Robertson. He cites increased productivity, decreased absenteeism, increased morale, and decreased recruiting costs as the selling points he uses to bring more businesses into the telecommuting fold. As usual, the bottom line won out.

Robertson says that once that shift occurred, the mind-set toward telecommuting shifted within Pacific Bell as well. In the beginning it was mostly managers who telecommuted at the company. But now Pacific Bell is starting to look at the possibility of having people in nonmanagement positions telecommute as well.

Instead of looking at the employee's rank, the company is starting to consider the types of jobs people do and to assess whether they really need to come into the office. "We need to look at the way we do business in a particular environment," says Robertson. "We've taken the same shift our customers have taken, so that it's no longer a legislation issue. Pacific Bell and other companies need to do this to stay competitive."

Why Businesses Don't Like Telecommuting

One of the biggest objections businesses have to telecommuting is the fact that they are unable to see their employees. Two factors will serve to make this less of a problem. First, as more and more employees telecommute, an increasing number of managers will adapt to managing by proxy. (To help your own manager manage you better when you work from home, see the section in chapter 7 called "Give This to Your Boss.") Second, the technology will continue to develop so that your boss will be able to view you in your home office, and you'll be able to see your boss as well. It's not videoconferencing per se, but the picturephones that futurists foresaw back in the 1960s are going to become more prominent as telecommuting and other remote work styles catch on.

Managers aren't crazy about telecommuting because they don't feel they will ever be able to fully trust their own employees. It's easy to spot supervisors of this type; they frequently sound as if they're talking to children when conversing with employees. They probably attended the heavy-handed school of management and believe strongly in the old adage that the mice will play when the cat's away (and figure that you do, too).

But I think the main reason businesses don't like telecommuting is that it's so different. There's really not much of a precedent managers and supervisors can use to tell them what to do and how to do it. They didn't learn how to manage by modem in business school, and they certainly didn't learn to place much emphasis on results; attendance and physical presence are the primary indicators of employee performance (still!) in the 1990s.

Also, many businesses don't like to give their own employees that much autonomy for fear that the workers might get confident about their abilities, might even go out one day, start their own businesses, and squire away a lot of the clients from their former employer. This is one reason why noncompete clauses are so prevalent these days, even among receptionists and secretaries. It's not just a matter of keeping your ex-employees from passing along secrets to your competition anymore; it's the fear that they'll actually become your competition!

However, even with all this gloom and doom, the environment in U.S. companies is actually getting better for telecommuting. Even though a lot of employees are afraid to suggest anything that might place them in jeopardy of losing their jobs, telecommuting is becoming so popular as a cost-cutting and productivity-increasing measure that workers may not have to muster up the nerve to ask their bosses if they can telecommute. Their bosses may beat them to it.

Telecommuting and the Law

Various states have enacted legislation that makes tele-commuting a good option for businesses. In California, for example, state law dictates that businesses having more than 100 employees in a single building must institute a plan to decrease the number of cars that drive to that location each day.

On November 15, 1994, the New Jersey Department of Transportation was swamped when more than 3,000 businesses having 100 or more employees were required to file trip-reduction plans detailing policies to reduce the total number of vehicles driven to and from the workplace each day. Though a department spokesman compared the deadline day to April 15, because so many plans were filed at the last minute, he said that most of the eligible companies were in compliance. If a firm neglected to submit these plans, the state could fine it $1,000 a month until the proposals were filed. The plans were required to be in place by November 1996. At that point the pressure on the businesses will intensify, because if the plans don't go into effect within two years after filing, New Jersey could lose up to $500 million in highway money from the federal government.

Illinois passed the Employee Commute Options Act in 1993 requiring companies in the Chicago area with—again—100 or more employees to cut the number of cars and other gasoline-powered vehicles that commute to one site between the hours of 6 and 10 A.M. Compliance is set for 1996. As in New Jersey, the cost of not going along with the law is steep: Penalties could amount to $10,000, plus a fine of $1,000 for each day that the company is in violation.

Of course, short of requiring employees to carpool, use public transportation in areas where service may be sparse, or come to work before 6 A.M. or after 10 A.M., one of the easiest and quickest solutions in response to legislative trip-reduction programs involves telecommuting. Even though one estimate put the number of Chicago-area telecommuters at 5,000 in 1993—an increase from 1,000 in 1990—businesses still have a long way to go to satisfy the law. Currently, the Chicago Telecommuting Advisory Council is exploring the option of adding more telecommuting centers in outlying areas as another way to help reduce inbound traffic.

Despite these moves, area officials admit that telecommuting has become popular more slowly in the Midwest than on either coast. Many Chicago-area managers believe that having some employees work from home is not entirely necessary, and companies often would rather try something else, such as staggered hours or additional shifts, before resorting to telecommuting. And even though a number of telecommuting programs in Chicago have shown sizable increases in productivity, managers initially don't believe the figures. In an article in *Crain's Chicago Business*, William Goodwin, the director of the Chicago Telecommuting Advisory Council, says that telecommuting "challenges so many myths about the business place. First, managers say, 'It doesn't make sense,' and then, after seeing [the] data, they say, 'It's too good to be true.'"

Congress got into the act in late 1994, when U.S. Representative Bill Baker (R–California) introduced a bill that would provide tax breaks to companies that allow their employees to telecommute. The proposed tax credit was pro-rated: If a worker telecommuted ten hours a week, the company would receive a $125 tax credit; a full-time employee telecommuting forty hours a week would earn his or her employer $500 in tax credits each year. Telecommuting centers were not viewed as highly in the bill, as employees using them still have to commute to some extent. An employee who works from a telecommuting center full-time would earn his or her employer $250 a year in tax credits. For big companies, of course, these savings add up. The bill, known as H.R. 3923, was introduced in the second half of the year, but it didn't go anywhere.

The federal government is encouraging telecommuting among some of its own employees. It instituted the Office of Workplace Initiatives in the General Services Administration branch and has set up four trial telecommuting centers outside of Washington, D.C., to enable some employees to eliminate their long commute into the city. Like other employers, the government is using such programs to reduce pollution, retain employees, and save money. Though the government has been studying telecommuting and other flexible work options as a way to cut costs and meet federal air-pollution mandates, the pilot program was put into motion only after officials discovered that the 700 federal employees who were already telecommuting were absent from work less often than their office-bound counterparts and displayed increased productivity.

Unions don't like telecommuting. Labor leaders feel that with more employees moving into home offices, and with fewer people working in factories today than ever before, unions will have a tougher time organizing workers and will lose members and, therefore, revenue. Much to the unions' dismay, antiquated home-work laws have been reversed in recent years as state and federal labor departments have witnessed the benefits of having some employees work at home. In 1942 the U.S. Department of Labor banned home knitters and other types of home workers because of the fear that small homes with one knitter each would eventually develop into sweatshops. Although there's no fear of that happening today, some unions are looking closely at the rise of telecommuters and thinking about starting a battle with the labor department about banning the home knitters all over again. They look at the sheer numbers of people who are working from home and immediately think about their declining memberships and budgets.

But they're looking at the wrong people. For one thing, telecommuters don't tend to work in fields that lend themselves to unionization. However misled by the new technology, though, the unions are not going to ignore the topic, and may decide to make it an issue by picking on the wrong group of employees—the home knitters.

PROFILE OF A TELECOMMUTING COMPANY: AT&T'S TELECOMMUTING DAY

On September 20, 1994, AT&T made history with its Telecommuting Day. More than 30,000 employees, representing 13 percent of the company's U.S. work force, worked from home for all or part of the day. Many lived in congested areas where commutes were typically horrendous affairs. Five hundred employees each in San Francisco and Detroit participated, as did 300 in southern Florida. The experiment was intended to promote telecommuting at AT&T as well as at other companies, which could realistically benefit from (and purchase) AT&T's products if their employees began to telecommute regularly. The company also wanted to use the event to see its telecommuting strengths and weaknesses. Chairman Robert E. Allen, who worked at home for the morning, told the *Wall Street Journal*, "I'll be at home for as long as I can stand it."

Telecommuting is not new to AT&T, however; approximately 22,500 employees already telecommute at least once a month. Two-thirds of these workers, however, are sales representatives, managers, and support workers.

More than three-quarters of the people who participated in Telecommuting Day said they were more productive; 23 percent worked out their participation with their managers in advance. In fact, this was one of the core issues AT&T wanted to examine in the context of Telecommuting Day. The company discovered that even though 20 percent of its employees telecommute at least once a month, only one-fourth of these had formal arrangements with their bosses; the rest stayed at home to work on an as-needed basis. One disadvantage of not drawing up formal proposals and agreements between telecommuting employees and their supervisors is that disagreements and misunderstandings can easily arise if there is nothing written down. AT&T plans to encourage even more employees, especially its managers, to make telecommuting a regular thing. But there's a long way to go. Even though the company seems gung-ho on the future of telecommuting, only about 60 percent of its employees say that their supervisors support the idea. The company plans to have more than half of its 60,000 managers in the United States telecommuting at least part-time by the year 2000.

When regular AT&T telecommuters were asked what they did with the time they saved by working at home, 32 percent said they spend it with their families, and 29 percent said they do more work. One-fifth said they use the time to run errands.

AT&T doesn't know if it will make Telecommuting Day an annual event, but the first one built huge awareness of this work option not only among its own staff but among employees at other companies as well. The company has invited executives at other firms to visit its main headquarters in New Jersey to find out how they can apply what AT&T has learned to their own companies.

The Benefits of Telecommuting

Companies that institute formal telecommuting policies often crow about it with a slew of press releases and claim they're doing it all for their employees. As we've already seen, however, it's usually money that really planted the seed. The profit motive, or fear of the law—don't forget the inevitable fines—is what really gets the ball rolling. Companies that address the issue of telecommuting soon discover a whole slew of goodies that come along for the ride. And, yes, these goodies all mean an improved bottom line. In short, telecommuting helps companies:

- Lower office expenses, including rent, utilities, and equipment
- Increase productivity
- Decrease employee turnover
- Meet Clean Air Act requirements
- Foster a more content work force
- Create jobs and equipment to meet the needs of telecommuters
- Become more competitive in the marketplace
- Show workers the employer cares about them
- Teach supervisors to exercise a more flexible management style
- Communicate with colleagues and managers in a more focused, concise way
- Enhance computer literacy (computerphobes at corporate headquarters become computer-literate if there are telecommuters around, especially if the telecommuter tends to communicate primarily by computer).

Though some telecommuters may not necessarily see this last point as a benefit, the fact that they are always near their computers means they can contact clients and colleagues in places several time zones away. Workers don't have to stay late at the office or arrive early for the sole purpose of communicating with someone far away. When expecting a call from Japan or from the West Coast, a worker can go into his or her home office at the appointed time, take care of the business, then resume the evening's activities.

Disadvantages of Telecommuting

Though telecommuting is often promoted as a way for companies to save money on rent and utilities, this argument usually only works on paper. The truth is that if you decide to work from home, even five days a week, your company will still have to pay for your former work space—unless your whole department starts to work from home full-time and your employer can close down the space. Even then, of course, there are expenses incurred in keeping an empty floor or building, unless the business rents it out or sells it.

Most companies realize this, which is why saving the expense of office space is rarely mentioned as the primary motivation for telecommuting anymore. Most often, other employees will simply spread out to assume some of your former space as their own. Real estate savings only play an important role in larger companies when enough employees are telecommuting on a regular basis that the business can close off a floor, lease out space to another business, or sell the building in total. However, some estimates suggest that companies can save up to $5,000 a year in office, parking, and utility costs.

According to Gil Gordon, who believes that no employee should be forced to telecommute, one disadvantage of telecommuting is that businesses can get greedy about the financial savings. "For example," says Gordon, "if an employer's sole motivation for looking at telecommuting is to save on rent and utilities, they may think if they can save a little bit of room and money by having some of their people telecommute part of the week, then they'll be able to save a ton of space and money by having almost all of their people telecommute almost all of the week." He doesn't agree: "The company then crosses over from having this be a good idea for some people to being a terrible idea that benefits hardly anybody."

Gordon cites a couple of clients who typified this penny-wise, pound-foolish thinking. "In one case the company saved $50 per telecommuter by not having fax capabilities built into the modems they gave their telecommuters to use at home, but they ended up creating all kinds of aggravation because the employees couldn't easily send faxes from their home offices," says Gordon. "The company then spent many times their savings in loss of effectiveness and aggravation from their employees. False economies can frequently undercut the benefits of telecommuting."

Getting Started

Telecommuting often gets its start at a company because of an exceptional case. For instance, if an employee who doesn't telecommute becomes temporarily disabled by injury or illness but is still able to work, he or she can usually continue to work to some extent from home with the right equipment. Because keeping busy helps people get better, a temporarily sidelined employee who telecommutes even part-time will often recuperate sooner, which means fewer medical bills and lower insurance premiums for her employer.

To get telecommuting off the ground, a company should initially plan for three stages. First, the employer needs to enable employees and managers to learn about telecommuting, either through briefings and meetings or through formal workshops and seminars conducted by an outside consultant. Next, many large companies start out with a relatively small pilot program in order to work out the kinks before they proceed to the third stage, a full-blown companywide program.

For his part, Gordon doesn't provide equipment or people to the companies he works with. Rather, he supplies the expertise to help companies implement a pilot or demonstration project in which a few employees work outside of the office for six months. "As a rule, companies tend to start off small," says Gordon. "There's usually someone in the middle of the organization who's a champion for telecommuting and tries to sell it within the company. This is the first hurdle, and it is sometimes as far as they get. It may take a mandate from the government—like a trip-reduction act—to attract the attention of the CEO. Then they'll sometimes collect a lot of information and try to implement it in-house within a short period of time. This can present a problem, however, because the middle managers haven't really been briefed, and if they're not for the program, they can easily but subtly sabotage the chance for telecommuting in the whole company for the near future."

Gordon says that in an ideal situation someone at or near the top of the corporate structure is pushing for telecommuting. "When someone in charge is for telecommuting, things can move very quickly. Then they sit down and plan for every detail about how the manager and the worker are going to work together while apart. What this does is help telecommuters become productive very quickly." He warns that if companies skip that step, the telecommuter and manager may bumble along; six months later they learn how to work at home by trial and error. Gordon says many corporations skip the middle-manager level when they first start to investigate telecommuting.

In addition, the company may hire a consultant—like Gordon—to assess the corporate structure and analyze how telecommuting could fit in. "I sit down with the managers in each department and ask them about their jobs and how much face-to-face contact they have with coworkers and clients," says Gordon. "I'll also ask them how much work they do over the telephone, by traveling, and by other means. Also, the number of people in the department is important; if there are only two, it might not work to have one of them out telecommuting."

He suggests that both managers and employees get very specific about how they're doing their work right now so that he can recommend different options that might work in a telecommuting situation.

"The sales department is the opening wedge to tele-commuting at most companies," says Gordon. "They already have notebook computers, and they've always been more mobile than other workers. And now they can get powerful notebook computers that can do fantastic presentations in a client's office that will blow away the competition. Then, when they get home, they can plug those computers in at night and completely update the inventory and cost so that they're updated in every department."

Gordon says telecommuting actually involves a kind of virtual office, which may be your car, your home, or even a restaurant. Labels such as "virtual office" will probably disappear as more people work with information and fewer work in the manufacturing fields, he adds.

A few companies decide to test telecommuting by first farming out work to home-based independent contractors. Then, when both the company and independent contractors express an interest in a full-time work arrangement, the employee doesn't start coming into the office every day. He or she continues to work at home. In an article in the December 1990 issue of *Nation's Business*, writer Michael

Alexander tells of a company that grew so fast in its early months that the president had no choice but to hire employees who telecommuted full-time. In fact, the rush that began when Danny McElroy first launched Carousel Mediaworks was so intense that he did not have time to rent office space and set up a real company. His employees didn't care, however. "Everyone likes it," McElroy told the magazine. "Early on I kept asking if we needed to get an office because I wanted to make sure that everyone was happy."

One employee left because the company was so busy that there wasn't time to schedule the regular weekly meeting for several weeks. McElroy did set up an e-mail system and a company bulletin board in addition to the weekly meetings, but this employee needed more in-person contact than the company's work required.

Some companies have begun telecommuting programs for unusual reasons. Ortho Pharmaceuticals set up a temporary telecommuting program while it searched for a bigger office space. Rather than continue with the squeezed conditions, Ortho sent half its employees home to work for half the week. Two officemates shared each desk and alternated working from home until the company moved into more spacious quarters.

The telecommuting program at Pacific Bell actually got its start during the 1984 Summer Olympics in Los Angeles. Many of the company's employees worked downtown, but the local government required many businesses to put their employees somewhere else for the duration of the games, so that the city's already famous traffic jams did not turn into monumental gridlock twenty-four hours a day. Pacific Bell had some of its employees work in the company's suburban offices. Others worked at home. The program was so successful that after the games ended, more than a few employees asked if they could continue telecommuting. A year later Pacific Bell got its experimental telecommuting program underway, and today it's an ingrained part of the company's work routine.

The Ten Best Companies for People Who Want to Telecommute

An article called "The Best Opportunities for Telecommuters" by Brad Schepp in the October 1990 issue of *Home Office Computing* listed the best companies for which to telecommute. These standings were based on both the number of employees who were telecommuting at the time of the survey and the potential for that number to grow. At each of these companies, the percentage of employees who telecommute grows every year without fail.

1. AT&T
2. Pacific Bell
3. California State Department of General Services
4. Apple Computer
5. County of Los Angeles
6. General Electric Plastics
7. The Federal Government
8. US West, Inc.
9. Travelers Corporation
10. J.C. Penney

Gil Gordon says Merrill Lynch, American Express, Nationwide Insurance, Sears, and some government agencies and phone companies are also beginning to rely on telecommuting more. In fact, he says, the types of companies that are instituting telecommuting have become increasingly diverse. It used to be concentrated in industries such as banking and insurance, but now it's really spreading out because the concept can be used in many more places than not, he says.

PROFILE OF A TELECOMMUTER: SUSAN HERMAN

Susan Herman is the general manager of the Department of Telecommunications for the City of Los Angeles. The department was created in 1985 to deal with various cable TV and franchising issues but is now charged with investigating telecommuting and devising strategic ways for the city government to utilize audio, video, data, and voice communications. The ultimate aim is to make Los Angeles a more attractive place to live and work.

Herman served as the chair of the 1985 city task force on telecommuting. The task force surveyed city employees, supervisors, elected officials, and other stakeholders in the region. From the information it gathered, the task force decided to do a pilot telecommuting project. The pilot involved 250 participants who were actively telecommuting and a control group of 250 other employees who worked for the same bosses as the telecommuters, did the same job, and had a similar commute to the office. To answer any questions or address problems, a telecommuting advocate was named in each department. Participants weren't allowed to telecommute less than one day a week, and an evaluation was required before an employee started telecommuting, midway through the pilot, and at the end. The program leaders took the same steps with the control group and conducted focus groups in between surveys.

Herman says this is where the city first found out about the tremendous benefits of telecommuting. City employees were 12½ percent more productive than their nontelecommuting counterparts; they were absent two days less per year; and they saved the city almost $8,000 a year per telecommuter. Almost 20 percent of the employees in the program said that being able to telecommute was a decisive reason why they stayed with their city job. Herman says an unexpected benefit was a 23 percent reduction in the personal use of employee vehicles.

"In fact, we found the program results were so sterling that we decided to expand the program to one-third of our total work force, or 15,000 out of 44,000 people," she says. "We are also looking at ways that people can make decisions that make telecommuting more effective. For example, many people are currently talking about having voice mail or call forwarding, since it would make their telecommuting more effective."

Herman says each telecommuter works from home an average of 1.4 days per week. "On any given day, you may have someone on their second day of telecommuting that week, while others choose to telecommute for three weeks once a quarter," she says. "We allow everyone to choose what makes the most sense for their work assignment that also takes into account their need for face to face interaction back at the office."

The day after the 1994 Northridge earthquake, Herman got busy. "First, we created a telecommuting partnership that involved five counties in Southern California and the City of Los Angeles on the public sector side and six private sector companies, including Pacific Bell, GTE, Intel, IBM, AT&T, and Northern Telecom. Then we created an 800 number that people could call in to get expert advice on any aspect of telecommuting," she says. She also assembled a list of vendors who could provide companies and employees with software, hardware, furnishings, and other items. The partnership also provided training, both on-site workshops and general seminars, and developed a curriculum of materials about telecommuting. "The easy thing back then was to advocate home-based telecommuting as a broad-based solution, but we also realized that there are people who need telework centers to go to work in lieu of their home or regular office," Herman notes. "Maybe they need more sophisticated equipment than they could get at home, or else they may not find their home environment to be conducive to telecommuting."

Before the quake, Herman says, the city operated six telework centers throughout the region. A year after the quake, there were twenty-three. All are being equipped with desktop videoconferencing, a conference room with videoconferencing facilities, copiers, fax machines, and both IBM and Macintosh computers, and they're all interconnected. You can link up with people at other centers.

According to Herman, these facilities were primarily developed by the public sector, though sometimes in partnership with private companies. "We decided to share facilities, because even though we may have a facility in Ontario, being able to have access to twenty-two other centers is fabulous," she says. "By sharing the wealth, we have a huge network. My employees don't come from just one region; they come from throughout Southern California."

Telecommuting Snapshot

In a study by the Gartner Group, 37 percent of telecommuters questioned worked for an employer with fewer than 5 employees; 19 percent worked at a company with five to nineteen workers; 21 percent worked at a company with 20 to 99 employees; 19 percent worked at businesses with between 100 and 999 employees; and a mere 4 percent worked for a company that had more than 1,000 employees.

(continued)

(continued)

Top Businesses for Telecommuting

Business services	12%
Retailing, wholesaling	11%
Banking, finance	11%
Manufacturing	9%
Telecommunications	6%
Health care	6%
Other services	5%
Transportation, utilities	4%
Real estate, insurance	3%
Government	3%
Other (arts, education, social or religious groups, agriculture)	30%

3

Are You Right for Telecommuting?

You may like the idea of telecommuting because you sense that it will change your lifestyle. And it probably will in a lot of good ways. But it will also bring a couple of inconveniences.

Not everyone was cut out to telecommute. In fact, the first group of people I can cite are those who want to work at home—or from a telework center—because they think they will be working less. Wrong. Telecommuting is not for people who think they'll be able to slack off. You may not work any extra hours—though, in fact, many people who telecommute do—but it's likely you'll work more intensely because you'll probably be interrupted less often at home than you would be in the office. This means you'll be able to concentrate more and work for longer periods of time. In fact, the time may fly by.

It's important to do a little bit of analysis on both your job and yourself before you even think about approaching your boss about telecommuting. The more clear you are in your reasons, the stronger your case will be when you present it for approval. And who knows? After reading this chapter, you may discover that telecommuting is *not* right for either you or your job.

Frank Damico of Bell Atlantic says a number of his employees have raised questions about telecommuting at the company. After researching it on their own, some of them decide that it's not right for them. "Some don't have the proper environment to work at home," says Damico, "but others just like the social interaction in the office and don't want to forgo that."

Why Do You Want to Telecommute?

People who are interested in telecommuting have their own reasons for wanting to work from home. Before you start to work on the logistics, you should evaluate exactly why you want to telecommute. If you do it for the wrong reasons—to get away from an abusive boss, for instance— the chances are good that you won't get the full benefit from working at home, as something other than your own desire is fueling it.

Even though you may already have a good idea of why you want to telecommute, answering the following questions will help you focus on your true motivations. It's a good idea to get a notebook at this time so you can start planning your telecommuting arrangement in detail. Throughout the book, I'll give you the opportunity to ask yourself about different aspects of telecommuting and show you how to draw up a proposal to convince your boss to let you work from home. Answer the questions honestly and include as much detail as you need. And keep your answers in mind as you read the chapters to come.

1. Why do you want to telecommute at your current job? Write down five answers and rank them in order of importance.

2. How many days a week do you think you'll want to work from home?

3. What do you like about your job?

4. What do you hate about your job?

5. What's your biggest excuse for not going ahead with plans to telecommute?

6. Describe how you envision a typical day that you'll spend working from home.

7. What kind of work would you choose to do if you worked at home one or more days a week?

8. Would you need to have some of your office responsibilities covered by another employee on the days when you're working from home?

9. Who would you call in the office if you needed some help or research done on the days you telecommute?

10. How much time each week do you spend commuting to the office? If you were working from home at least part of the time, how would you regard those extra hours: as time to use for yourself, or as more time to spend working?

11. Do you feel comfortable working by yourself for an entire day? What would you do if you felt that you needed some kind of social contact?

Are You Cut Out for Telecommuting?

No matter how much you may think you want to work from home, the truth is that you just may not be cut out for it. Answering the following questions will help you find out:

1. Does your boss show that he trusts you completely?

2. Do you have a good track record when it comes to meeting deadlines and producing sufficient work?

3. Are you able to motivate yourself, or do you need someone to tell you what to do?

4. Do you consider yourself fairly well organized?

5. Are you comfortable with your job and its responsibilities?

6. Do you basically get along with your coworkers? If there's someone you don't particularly care for, will working from home improve the relationship or make it worse?

7. Are you flexible when it comes to priority projects?

8. Are you able to work by yourself most of the time?

9. Are you able to communicate your needs clearly to your coworkers?

10. Can you avoid becoming a workaholic, which would leave even less time for yourself?

If you answered "no" to more than half of these questions, you had better give more thought to the downside of telecommuting before you invest any time in setting up your home office.

Is Your Job Right for Telecommuting?

Basically, the types of jobs that are best suited for telecommuting include:

☐ Jobs that require frequent use of the telephone

☐ Jobs that don't rely on in-person contact

☐ Jobs where most of the work is done on computers

☐ Jobs that deal with a series of projects that have definite beginnings and endings

☐ Jobs that can be done in a small, possibly confined area

☐ Jobs that don't rely on constant feedback from coworkers

☐ Jobs where tasks can be done by one employee or combined with the work of other employees at a later date

Let's assume that you want to telecommute, your job is suited for it, and your supervisor agrees. You should still investigate if there are any technicalities that will hinder your plan. For instance, if you work for a public utility company, a picky residency requirement may get in your way. Such a regulation applies to operating telephone companies (OTCs). An OTC can only legally conduct business within its own jurisdiction. As stipulated in the "Telecommuter Pre-Screen Process" workbook published by Bell Atlantic for its employees, if you work for Bell of Pennsylvania but live in New Jersey, for instance, you cannot telecommute. This seems unfair, especially since Bell Atlantic, the parent company, covers New Jersey, Pennsylvania, and several other states. But that is the law.

However, there's a strange little twist to this. Scattered throughout the country are small, independent telephone companies, mostly in rural areas, that usually cover a portion of a state. If you are a Bell Atlantic employee that happens to live in an area served by an independent telephone company, but the state as a whole is served by Bell Atlantic, you will be able to telecommute because the area where you live—and will work from your home office—is covered.

Job Tasks Worksheet

You might have the temperament to work at home, and your boss might be in agreement, but the best way to determine whether or not telecommuting is the best choice for you is to break down the specific types of tasks you perform regularly for your job. Then analyze them in terms of the equipment you'll have at your disposal at home.

The following chart was filled out by an employee at Bell Atlantic as part of the telecommuting pre-screening process utilized by the company:

Job Tasks	Phone	PC	Printer	Modem	Fax	At Home?
Reading						Yes
Writing		Yes	Yes			Yes
Programming	Yes	Yes	Yes	Yes		Yes
Client Contact	Yes				Yes	Yes
Planning		Yes	Yes			Yes
Sales	Yes	Yes	Yes	Yes	Yes	Yes
Desktop Publishing		Yes	Yes		Yes	Yes
Supervising/ Managing	Yes	Yes			Yes	Yes
Training						

If you'd like to conduct a similar exercise, start by naming all the responsibilities you have in your job, as shown under "Job Tasks" in the Bell Atlantic chart. Then list the common types of equipment you normally use when performing these tasks. Compare this equipment with each job task and answer "yes" in the appropriate spots.

The final question, of course, is whether or not you can do the tasks your job requires with the equipment you have at home. If not, you and your employer will have to determine if you can perform these tasks on the days you spend in the office or if the projected increase in your productivity would warrant the expense of outfitting your home office with the necessary equipment.

Eight Reasons Why Employees Don't Telecommute, Even When They Want to Do So

1. They're afraid they'll come back to no job.
2. They think they can't afford to telecommute.
3. They think their arch rival at the company is going to leap ahead in their absence.
4. They think they'll be out of sight, out of mind.
5. They believe it will hold them back in the future when it comes to raises and promotions.
6. They don't have any idea what they'd do with all that free time.
7. The economy's shaky, and they'll be among the first to go in case of a layoff.
8. Other employees will think of them as uncommitted and disloyal, and they'll be left out of the corporate culture.

Eight Reasons Why Employees Decide to Telecommute

1. They need a break from the Monday-through-Friday grind, and a two-week vacation just won't cut it. What's needed is a permanent change in their work style.

2. They want to spend time with their families, as in the good old days.

3. They want to learn a new skill, such as a new language or an art form, with the new free time they'll have.

4. They're sick of long commutes.

5. They want to reduce the amount of stress in their lives.

6. They need to save money, and one way to do so is to eliminate or reduce commuting costs.

7. They're tired of being constantly interrupted at work and having to take their work home anyway to do at night.

8. They'll quit if they don't change their job in some way.

Why Do You Think Telecommuting Will Work for You?

It's important that you consider telecommuting in a nonlinear fashion. Unless you spend all of your work time doing one task or you want to work from home five days a week, break down your job into separate responsibilities to see which tasks are better done from home and which require you to be in the office. You don't need to justify your entire job in order to convince your boss to let you telecommute. Many jobs today consist of just three operational tasks: preparation, production, and presentation. Break your job down into these categories. For many people, any preparation work can be done at home, especially if it doesn't require input from outside people. As for the production stage, parts of it can usually be done at home, whereas other tasks involve research that is more easily done in the office. The presentation stage is usually the shortest of the three, and is usually done in a professional setting: your company office or the office of a client.

If you have several projects in different stages going on at the same time, you often can consolidate the tasks in the production and preparation stages and complete them on the two or three days a week that you choose to work from home.

Consultant Joanne Pratt says that people who are in managerial positions and typically spend a lot of time processing information have the greatest chance of success at telecommuting because a lot of their work can be done at a desk. "In most of these jobs, there's one or two days' worth of work that can be better done away from the interruptions of the on-site office," she says. "Manufacturing is least conducive to telecommuting, whether you work on an assembly line or in the office of a manufacturing plant where there's only a couple of employees and they all need to be there!"

Jack Robertson of Pacific Bell says the technical end of telecommuting is actually the easiest to handle, which is why his company will usually deal with it last. "There are very few technical reasons why we can't make most people work remotely if they're some kind of an information worker," he says. "After all, we are the phone company. But once we get you past the point of dealing with the human resources issues, then we'll address the technology. If we address the technology first and somebody's still nervous about it, you'll never get through to the technological part anyway."

What if Telecommuting Is Mandatory?

Although experts advise that both the company and employees more fully benefit from telecommuting if it is instituted on a voluntary basis, a small but growing number of companies are requiring their employees to telecommute. In programs where telecommuting is mandatory, supervisors will usually meet to discuss which employees would benefit most from telecommuting. However, they usually don't base the decision on temperament. Instead, the gauge used is the amount of time you already spend away from the office. If you already spend three out of five days on the road, managers charged with implementing telecommuting at their companies will think, "Why does he or she need an office?"

One telecommuting experiment at an IBM office in Indiana showed that only about 17 percent of telecommuters disliked the hoteling concept and wanted to return to a more traditional situation. Analysts say the people who spent less than 60 percent of their time out of the office were most unhappy with the situation.

Telecommuting Snapshot

Here's how 100 telecommuters describe the type of job they do:

Sales	12%
Business professional	11%

(continued)

(continued)	
Programmer, technician	10%
Executive, manager	8%
Engineer, scientist	7%
Teacher	6%
Health-care professional	5%
Lawyer, accountant, consultant	4%
Government, public sector	4%
Arts, music	4%
Construction	4%
Precision production	2%
Clerical	1%
Other	22%

Telecommuting Is Not for Everyone

People who tend not to thrive on telecommuting include employees who have conflicts at home and people who need an outside source of motivation. Social butterflies generally don't do well in the context of telecommuting, as the isolation inherent in working at home can be so distracting that they aren't able to get any work done. The key is not to rely heavily on e-mail as opposed to regular voice contact; whether they're at home or in the office, employees should make a point to call each other regularly.

Many experts recommend that an employee work for at least a year with a company before even broaching the idea of telecommuting, but some firms set new employees up at home immediately. A public relations company in San Francisco called Primetime Publicity and Media employs fifteen people; one-third of them telecommute, including several new employees.

It's also been suggested that telecommuting does not work for mothers and/or fathers looking to bypass child-care costs (this works to some extent, but not fully) or people who have had problems with drug or alcohol addiction in the past. Single people who look to the workplace for a good part of their social life will also do a better job if they work in the office at least three or four days a week. If one or more of the following applies to your home environment, then telecommuting may not be a good choice for you:

- ☐ Feelings of isolation
- ☐ Easy access to the refrigerator
- ☐ A noisy neighborhood
- ☐ Family or friends who interrupt
- ☐ Omnipresent television

How Telecommuting Will Affect Your Career

You're starting to think about taking time off, even starting to fantasize about how you're going to spend that big uninterrupted block of time, when, suddenly, reality interferes:

"What will this do to my career?"

It can only harm it, you think, and so you replace thoughts of working from home with thoughts about the long commute home and the microwaved dinner. You start to close this book . . . WAIT!

It's entirely possible that deciding to telecommute won't affect your climb up the corporate ladder, though you may have to work a bit harder to stay visible in people's minds back at the office. Telecommuting might even help you get where you want to go a bit faster. One thing's for sure: Making the decision to telecommute won't get you demoted unless it was inevitable anyway. And in that case, why would you want to continue working for a company that doesn't care whether or not its employees are happy?

PROFILE OF A TELECOMMUTER: TAKY TZIMEAS

Taky Tzimeas is a detective supervisor who's been with the Los Angeles Police Department since 1974. From 1991 to 1994 he telecommuted on a regular basis while working in the Internal Affairs Department (IAD), where Tzimeas was assigned to the Rodney King investigation. During that time he worked eighty to eighty-five hours a week for ten weeks and had so many reports to review and write that he would work on them at his home, which was 25 miles from the office. "I could stay home and work on them because on certain days there was simply no need for me to go into office and review them."

Although he worked these six- and seven-day weeks for just over three months, Tzimeas appreciated the fact that he could stay at home and work. "In fact, my supervisor told me in advance that if I knew I would be doing nothing but reviewing documents, I could work from home and save two hours of commuting time a day. This benefited both the city and me, as I was able to catch up on sleep and work instead of spending those two hours driving." If the office needed to get in touch with him, Tzimeas's supervisor would call him by phone or over a pager. Likewise, he would call or beep them whenever he needed to discuss aspects of the case.

After the Rodney King case ended, Tzimeas stayed with the IAD reviewing other cases. "In any given month, we'd have a couple hundred cases to review," he says. "Some of the more serious or complex cases could run 200 pages or more. We didn't need to be in the office to review them, so my partner and I would each take one or two days a week and telecommute from home. Then we'd write up a synopsis of each case and present that report to the police commission along with our evaluation."

Tzimeas says he didn't need a computer because this aspect of his work was pretty much self-contained. And if he did need additional resources, they were only as far away as his phone. "Having a computer in the main office was a major help because if I was writing reports all day long, I could write it by hand at home and then have the secretaries at the office type the written reports," he says. "However, if you need other sources or need to jump on a computer program or search through files, those types of jobs don't lend themselves to telecommuting. And if you do skimp on the additional information, you may be shortchanging your job by not consulting those resources you need."

Tzimeas found that in a normal day he'd do approximately eight to twelve case reviews at home. Without any interruptions, from the phone ringing or people asking for advice, he was able at least to double his productivity. He also put out a much better product. "In fact, I loved it so much that I'd put in more than eight hours each day to ensure that our productivity at work would increase."

Tzimeas says that when he started to work from home, it shocked the heck out of his dog and cat. "It was wonderful to be able to throw on anything and just lounge-lizard around my own home all day," he says. "I didn't have to shave, and I could immediately start working and be able to concentrate without having constant noise in the background. It's hard to concentrate for more than two to five minutes at the station without interruptions. At home, I could work in thirty-minute bites, which allowed me to really get into the analysis of a case." He also liked the fact that he could drink his own coffee and follow a regular exercise schedule. "I try to work out five days a week, and telecommuting was great, because after sitting there working for four hours, my mind started to tie into knots. I have a gym at home, so I could work out and come back all sweaty and either get right back into a case or take a shower. I needed those mental breaks from work when I telecommuted," he says. He's able to switch back and forth, but some people aren't. "If you would just muddle through your job at home without supervision, then telecommuting is not for you.

"At work if someone calls and you chitchat for fifteen minutes, you don't feel guilty. But if you're working at home, the exact opposite is true: if the phone rings and it's a personal phone call, you have to keep reminding yourself you're at work. You feel like you're cheating when you're not putting the nose to the grindstone when you're telecommuting. I think this is what helps contribute to the productivity."

In 1995 Tzimeas switched to an assignment that didn't lend itself to telecommuting. "The type of job I have now is more interactive, so I think I'd miss the people. In the other job I wanted to put an isolation dome over my head in order to concentrate. But I'd love to go back to telecommuting, to be in an assignment where it would be possible."

Telecommuting Snapshot

- □ Eighty-three percent of telecommuters work at home part-time, which is considered less than thirty-five hours a week.
- □ Thirty-three percent work at home one day each week.
- □ Seventy-seven percent of telecommuters work at companies that have fewer than 100 employees.
- □ In 1995, 51 percent of telecommuters were men, and 49 percent were women; 34 percent made under $35,000, and 34 percent made between $35,000 and $75,000.

4

How to Negotiate with Your Boss

Employees often avoid pursuing a telecommuting lifestyle for fear of their boss's reaction. However, some experts believe it's easier to deal with a boss's concerns than with a potential telecommuter's logistical problems. Why? Because the concerns of most supervisors usually amount to a one-note song: "How can I manage an employee who I can't see? How do I know if the person is working or not?"

I'll deal with this issue later in the chapter, but I'll give you a hint: Managers all over the country are dealing with telecommuters by changing their managerial styles to focus on results instead of attendance. An employee that is present and accounted for isn't necessarily going to be productive. On the contrary, we've all known employees who not only like to interrupt other workers but whose very presence and manner are disruptive in the extreme. In an article on telecommuting in the October 1994 issue of *PC World*, Michael Steward, an educational development manager for California's Pacific Bell, says that anyone who is interested in telecommuting should first point to the disruptive in-house employee who never seems to get much work done and interferes with colleagues' work as well. Once you remind your manager about all the losers he or she has had to supervise in the past, Steward believes, he or she will be more likely to evaluate performance on results instead of presence.

Making the First Move

Approaching your boss and asking to work a little bit differently from how the company's employees have always worked may well be the most difficult part of the entire telecommuting process for you. In fact, making the adjustment from working in a regular office to working from home may be simple once you get the okay. But even the most hard-nosed boss may assent to your request if you point out the benefits that the company will reap if you work out of your home either full- or part-time.

Some employers are naturally more amenable than others to granting flexible working arrangements. Obviously, the more valuable you are to your company, the more likely your boss will be to give you what you want. Creative businesses, industries that normally employ a large stable of freelancers, and businesses that require a good deal of quiet, concentrated work tend to be among the more telecommuter-friendly fields. In industries that operate on a project-by-project basis, an employee can easily work on research and preparation at home and come in to the office for stages that require more interaction with coworkers.

In order to convince your boss to let you telecommute at least a day or two each week, it's necessary to explain how it will benefit both you and the company. Therefore, you have to do your homework and take a very proactive stance right from the start.

Because many managers still resist the notion that employees can be productive in a setting other than a formal corporate workplace, it's important to stress the benefits your company will reap if you are allowed to telecommute.

For example, you might cite the fact that many studies have shown that telecommuting clearly cuts down on employee attrition; the flexibility inherent in telecommuting means that workers will have more time for their personal lives, increasing their loyalty to their employers. A business that has either an informal or a formal telecommuting policy, as well as other flexible work options, will find itself with very dedicated employees. Workers will work that much harder because they're grateful for the opportunity to work at home

It doesn't hurt if you're invaluable to the company. You stand the best chance of getting your company to agree to your desire to telecommute if you're an employee the company doesn't want to lose. It also helps if you've regularly pitched in beyond what was expected of you and if other workers regularly turn to you for advice on business and personal matters. Of course, your boss may say you're too valuable *in* the office to work outside of it, but you can always counter this argument by asking what it would be like at the office if you decided to leave permanently.

Sometimes, a telecommuting arrangement may start out as a temporary solution to a problem at the office. An employee on maternity leave or on medical disability may not be able to work full-time or commute into the office, but he or she may be able to work a few hours a day from home just to keep a finger in the pie. A supervisor may take on some of the absent worker's traditional job responsibilities and assign the rest, preferably the ones that need to be performed in the traditional office setting, to a coworker or two until the employee on leave can return. Both management and employees tend to like this arrangement; the

How to Negotiate With Your Boss

employee doesn't feel totally out of touch with the office for an extended period of time, and the manager won't have to hire someone new, which will help the company's bottom line.

Approaching Your Boss

The first thing you should do is tell your immediate supervisor you've been thinking about working from home a day or two a week. Don't make a big deal out of it; just mention it casually, allow him or her to react and then say something like, "I've worked it all out, and I'll drop off the details later in the week." Then change the subject. Your boss might say, "You must be kidding," or "Great, I'll be looking for it." The important thing at this stage is not to let the initial reaction kill your enthusiasm.

A few days later drop off your proposal, and stick around while your boss reads it. Then be prepared for any questions. Try not to get defensive if you are told it's impossible. Stay calm and reinforce your convictions by stressing how your telecommuting will benefit the company. If the answer is still no, try again in a few weeks, and let your boss know that you're serious.

It's not a good idea to go over the head of your immediate supervisor. It can create big problems down the road if your boss's supervisor says yes after your boss has said no. Offer to compromise on the number of days you want to telecommute, or toss in some other sweeteners that will convince him or her to say yes. One of two things will happen: You'll wear your boss down after awhile, when he or she sees that you're not going to give up, or your boss will find some excuse to fire or demote you so you're not a

78

problem anymore. Though you may not want this outcome, it will allow you to look for another job where you *will* be allowed to telecommute.

The most important thing an employee can do is to go to the manager with a definite plan. The worst thing you can do is to approach your boss unprepared, state that you want to telecommute, and ask, "Can you help me?" If the employee is willing to be flexible and comes in with a well-thought-out plan, the manager and the company will be more likely to work things out.

Planning Your Attack

Telecommuting consultant Joanne Pratt suggests that employees who want to convince their employer to let them telecommute start by writing an outline. "Include last month's calendar and offer an analysis of your work by pointing out which days you needed to be in the office for meetings and which days you could have worked from home," she says. "You need to get very specific and describe what your office at home looks like, what kinds of equipment you have and what you'll need, whether your office has a door, and how you're going to arrange for child care, if needed. In short, you should describe your working environment in a very professional manner. If you need to get equipment from the company, tell specifically where you're going to get it; for example, you know there is a spare 386 computer in a particular department because someone recently upgraded to a 486." Add that if you can have it on loan for your home office, it won't cost the company anything, Pratt says; companies like these kind of specifics.

Pratt suggests that you next outline the type of work you'll be doing from home, whether it's writing proposals or reports, reading, or making phone calls. Point out how you'd be more productive working from home and how you'd work with coworkers. "Develop as solid a presentation as you can in order to allay the fears not only of your supervisor but also of all those people your supervisor reports to," she says. "Basically, they want to know that they'll still be in control if you want to telecommute."

Then you'll want to put the request in the form of a written proposal.

Building Your Case

I cannot stress this point enough: When planning to telecommute, do your homework in advance. You must be able to convince your boss that telecommuting will benefit the company. Answer the following questions in your notebook, and here, especially, try to anticipate every move your boss will make in order to prepare your own response.

1. How do you think your boss will react to your request to telecommute? How can you prepare in advance for your meeting?

2. How willing are you to negotiate for time? If you ask to work from home three days a week and your boss offers one day a week to start, would you be willing to accept this?

3. How can you present telecommuting as a benefit to the company?

4. Will your absence on any particular day negatively affect the business in any way? What can you do to temper this?

5. Will the boss be more amenable to your request if you agree to keep in touch with the office a certain number of times a day?

6. What sweeteners can you guarantee the company if you're allowed to telecommute (i.e., any new knowledge that will help to increase productivity)?

Covering at the Office

Your boss will be much more likely to allow you to telecommute if you explain that on the days you're working from home no one will notice you're gone; the office will run that smoothly without you. Such reassurance will also endear you to your coworkers, who may fear that some of your work will be added to their already heavy workloads when you're out of the office.

One of the first things you can do is choose to telecommute on a naturally slow day at the office—that is, if one exists. It will also help if you can do some of the work ahead of time, spending an extra hour or two at the office each day to plan for future projects or get started on them.

If you have a secretary or administrative assistant, you may want to show him or her how to deal with potential problems that might arise in your absence. You can't give everyone in the office permission to call you when the tiniest problem comes up, or you might almost feel that you're back at the office, with all the interruptions decreasing your concentration and productivity. But sometimes your aide may have to call you. He or she will probably appreciate the extra responsibilities and the faith you place in him or her. It's a good idea to ask your assistant to list projects that he or she can do while you're out of the office.

Of course, you have to convince your manager that your assistant will be able to handle anything that comes up on days that you're telecommuting. If necessary, you can assuage the company's concerns by arranging to call in twice a day or so to check up on your assistant's progress and answer any questions that may come up.

Anticipating Your Company's Response

Even though you think you may know your boss, it's nearly impossible to predict precisely how he or she will react to your request to telecommute. It never hurts to do your homework and get a sense of how the company has treated other employees who have worked from home in the past. Write your answers to the following questions in your notebook.

1. How do you think your boss will respond when you ask to work from home?

2. Has the company ever allowed other employees to telecommute in the past? Can you find out the specifics? How did the employee approach the company? How many days a week did he or she telecommute, and for what purpose? Also, at what level of the company hierarchy was the employee?

3. Can you locate an employee who wanted to telecommute but was turned down? Again, find out the details. If the employee has since quit, try to track him or her down.

4. Does your company have a soft spot? You might want somehow to stress this aspect of telecommuting—you'll save the company money, you'll free up office space—when you approach your boss and write your proposal.

Your Proposal

No matter what form you use to present your proposal, here are the basic points you should cover:

1. Why do you want to telecommute?

2. How many days a week do you want to work from home? Will they stay the same each week, or will they vary depending on your workload?

3. What kind of equipment do you need?

4. Which tasks are you going to work on from home?

5. Will you need a separate phone?

6. Do you view this as a permanent or temporary work style?

7. How will you keep in touch with the office?

8. Who will cover for you at the office?

You'll also want to make sure that your proposal answers the following questions, especially if you need to present it to hard-headed number crunchers looking for a bottom-line benefit:

1. Why will this help the company?

2. How much money do you project it will save the company?

3. Why do you need to do something different from what everyone else at the company is doing?

4. Will any of your job responsibilities change? Will the time at which you carry them out change?

5. Will your department head and coworkers need to do anything differently? How will you help them?

6. Why is your job ideal for performing from home?

7. How will you and your supervisor evaluate your progress?

Put your answers to these questions in your proposal as well:

1. When do you want to start working from home? Why is that a good time?

2. What will you need to do to get ready so that you can work at home?

3. How often will you provide the company with details on whether or not telecommuting is successful for you? How early?

4. How much money do you think is needed to get started?

Other things you might also want to address, depending upon your individual situation, include who's going to handle child care while you're working from home, what kind of space you're going to be working in, and who's going to be responsible for maintaining the equipment you'll use at home.

The total proposal can be set down in a page or two, with each point succinctly covered. However, you should do as much additional research as possible so you can answer any other questions that may pop up.

When drawing up your proposal, it's important to include your company's mission statement, motto, or stated philosophy somewhere near the top. Your telecommuting arrangement may be doomed if you stray from the company's primary goals.

You might also want to speculate on whether you might decide to stop your telecommuting at some point in the future and for what reasons. Though it's hard to get a lock on it right now before you test yourself and your company, you'll need to troubleshoot your work-at-home arrangement from the very beginning and bring things back in line in the event they begin to stray.

Though in most cases telecommuting will have no effect on your pay scale and benefits package, you should state clearly in your proposal something to this effect. No more than a sentence is warranted. Some employees, either before or after they start to telecommute, begin to see that they want some additional flexibility in their jobs, perhaps in the form of fewer hours, and so compensation will naturally decrease in the transition from a full- to part-time job.

The proposal should spell out the length of your probationary period, during which you and your supervisor will analyze whether or not your telecommuting is working for you, the company, and your coworkers. You also should specify how often regular reviews will be held if you decide to continue telecommuting beyond the probationary period. It may work to your advantage to have performance reviews more often than your colleagues simply because you do require special attention. It's important that you maintain contact with your supervisor as to the progress you're making even though you don't fit the profile of other employees at the company.

You may need to prove to your boss that you can do your job at home as well as or better than in the office. You're more likely to convince your boss if you have a good track record of producing results in your job and if you can provide concrete examples that show you work better by yourself than with other employees and managers around. You may also want to cite projects you've completed successfully with a minimum of supervision to show that you can manage your time effectively, especially under tight deadlines.

If your manager doubts his or her ability to supervise you from afar, you may have to point out specific instances in which you worked on projects without direct oversight or in which your boss managed you in a slightly unorthodox fashion. Prove that he or she has a special talent for managing employees and keeping track of the progress of certain projects, and promise to provide your supervisor with checklists and other indicators of your productivity. Training can help, and if your company offers special seminars on telecommuting to both managers and employees, then you should both take advantage of them. But in the end, an effective relationship between supervisor and telecommuter requires trust. Who knows? Your work may be so impressive that your supervisor will want to start telecommuting, too.

In your proposal, you'll want to stress the benefits for your company—increased profits in the form of your improved productivity and the company's reduced office rent and utility costs. You should also use the current situation at your company to persuade your supervisor and his or her supervisors. Is employee retention a problem at your company? Could your company use some extra office space?

You'll also want to help your boss analyze your plan to telecommute. These are some of the questions he or she should ask before allowing you or any other employee to telecommute:

□ Is this employee the right kind of worker to telecommute?

- ☐ Does the job lend itself to telecommuting?

- ☐ Can I learn to manage telecommuters without regular face-to-face contact?

- ☐ Can I help my telecommuters to deal with the downside of working at home?

You may even want to frame the issue this way: As a telecommuter, you will in essence be your own manager, which can take some of the pressure off of your boss.

Your Telecommuting Agreement

Once your boss has given you the go-ahead, the two of you will probably have to sign a document that spells out the terms of your telecommuting arrangement. It might have to be approved by a member of your company's human resources department, if a staff member from that department was involved in the negotiating process.

What follows is a sample telecommuting agreement that provides for most of the details you'll have to keep in mind when working from home. Such a document may have to be altered as time goes on—for example, if you decide to increase the number of days you work from home or if you need to replace one piece of equipment with another.

Some of the details included here won't apply to you, and you may think of others that you need to insert into the document. You'll probably want to attach some of the checklists that appear elsewhere in this book to this agreement as a way to underscore the details.

Telecommuting Agreement

The following document will serve as an agreement between _____ (the employee) and _____ (the manager) at _____ (the company) in regard to a telecommuting work arrangement—including work schedule, equipment used, and other details—that will begin the week of _____ (the date).

1. The employee plans to work off-site at _____
_____ (location).

2. The employee plans to work off-site according to the following schedule: _____
_____ (days, hours, weeks, months).

3. The employee requires the use of the following equipment in order to do the work satisfactorily: _____

_____

_____

4. When working off-site, the employee will keep in touch with his or her supervisor and coworkers at the office in the following ways: _____

_____

_____

(continued)

(continued)

5. The employee will focus on the following work tasks when working from home: _____

_____

_____

_____

6. If the employee requires an additional telephone line, the monthly connection costs, long-distance charges, plus any special services (call waiting, call forwarding, voice mail, etc.) will be paid for by _____

7. The supervisor will determine the employee's progress on work completed at home through _____

_____

_____

_____

(number of phone calls, pages read or written, hours spent working, etc.)

8. The employee will participate in meetings and conferences held in the office in his or her absence through _____

_____

_____

_____

(teleconferencing, videoconferencing, the receipt of minutes, etc.)

(continued)

(continued)

9. The employee and supervisor will meet _____
_____
(how often) to monitor the telecommuting arrangement.

10. Other stipulations of this telecommuting work
arrangement: _____
_____
_____
_____

I agree to the conditions set forth in this agreement.

_____   _____
Employee   Date

_____   _____
Supervisor   Date

Anticipating Details

Before you start to telecommute, you must get very specific about not only the tasks you're going to do at home but also the manner and the work space in which you're going to do them. In other words, you'll have to examine your home office with an eye for everything from checking that a courier from one of the express delivery services knows which door to enter to making sure that the wiring in your house can handle the increased demand for electricity that your business equipment will place on it.

Not everything on the following checklist will apply to you—and you may think of a few details that apply to you that aren't on the list—but this will help you to get an overview of how telecommuting will affect your home life and your working life.

Model Telecommuting Checklist

Date _____

Name _____

Address _____

_____

Phone _____

Married or single? _____

Does your spouse work at home? _____

Do you have kids at home? How many? _____

Do you have any relatives or friends living with you?

When are they typically at home? _____

(continued)

(continued)

Describe your residence. Is it an apartment or a single-family home? How many square feet is it? Do you have a separate room for your home office? Does your home office have its own separate entrance? _____

_____

_____

_____

Describe the space you will be using for your home office. Will it be used for any other purpose besides your work? If so, what? _____

_____

Can you lock the door? Can you lock the windows? _____

_____

What kind of lighting is available for the room? Will you need to purchase new lamps or have an overhead fluorescent fixture installed? Who will pay for it? _____

_____

What office supplies will you need? Who will pay for it?

_____

_____

_____

(continued)

(continued)

Where are the electrical sockets located? Will you need to use an extension cord or electrical strip? _____

_____

Do you already have storage space in the office, such as a file cabinet, bookcases, a closet, or built-in bookshelves?

_____

Where will you store backed-up floppy disks or external hard drives? Will the storage area be safe from flooding, fire, and break-ins? _____

Is your planned home office space in the basement? If the basement tends to get damp, do you have a dehumidifier?

_____

Do you have a personal computer that you already use at home? What type of computer is it? Will you be using it to do your office work? Will you need to upgrade it in any way? If so, who will pay for the upgrade? _____

_____

_____

Do other people in your household use the computer? Will you need to put a stop to this once you start working from home? _____

_____

(continued)

(continued)

What type of software do you have on your home computer? Are the programs compatible with the software you use at work? If you need to transfer office files to your home computer, will your personal computer be able to support them? _____

_____

_____

Do you currently have any other kind of office equipment in your home? Is it sufficient for the tasks you'll need to do for your office work? _____

_____

_____

What type of desk will you be using? Is the one you currently have large enough for your office work? Will you need to get another one? Who will pay for it? _____

_____

_____

Does your computer at home have a modem installed on it? Do you need to put one on it? Who will pay for it? ____

_____

_____

_____

(continued)

(continued)

Are there phone jacks installed in the room you've designated for your home office? If not, can you run an extension from a nearby room? Do you need to have the phone company come and install a separate line? _____

_____

_____

Is your number listed or unlisted? Do you have an answering machine? Do you have a fax machine that can share a phone line, or do you need to install a second phone line to support a dedicated fax? _____

_____

_____

Do you have a smoke detector in the room you plan to use for your office? Does it run off of a battery, or is it hard-wired? When was the last time the smoke detector was inspected? _____

_____

_____

Do you have a fire extinguisher located in the office? When was it last inspected? _____

_____

_____

(continued)

(continued)

In case of fire, what is the best escape route from your home office? _____

_____

_____

What type of insurance do you have for your home? Do you need to have additional insurance to cover your home office? Will your current underwriter make the addition to your policy, or do you have to go to another insurance company? Will your company pay for additional coverage?

_____

_____

_____

_____

Will you be using your car for your work at home in any way? If so, do you need to get additional coverage on your automobile insurance policy? Who will pay for it? _____

_____

_____

Who should be contacted in case of an emergency at your home office?

Relative and phone number _____

_____

(continued)

(continued)

Neighbor and phone number _____

_____

Friend and phone number _____

_____

What entrance will you and others use to gain access to your home office? Is your house relatively easy to locate by delivery people? Is the entrance well-lit, and is your house number easily visible from the road? _____

_____

_____

_____

_____

If you're not at home, can packages be left on a porch or front step? If not, name a neighbor (with address) who will accept deliveries. _____

_____

_____

Who is responsible for keeping the entrance clear? _____

_____

_____

(continued)

(continued)

What do you need to do before you can begin to work in your home office? Set a deadline by which you plan to accomplish each step:

1. _____

Date _____

2. _____

Date _____

3. _____

Date _____

4. _____

Date _____

5. _____

Date _____

6. _____

Date _____

7. _____

Date _____

8. _____

Date _____

9. _____

Date _____

10. _____

Date _____

A Word of Warning

One problem you may find in negotiating is that if your boss is sixty or older, you may be coming up against some heavily ingrained biases against working from home. You may not be able to change these preconceptions no matter how many supportive statistics you provide.

Paul and Sarah Edwards, home-office consultants and authors of several books about working from home, write a question-and-answer column in *Home Office Computing* magazine. In the March 1995 issue they offer an interesting perspective on the generational differences in people's attitudes toward working at home. The Edwardses describe an incident in which Paul spoke to the Los Angeles Planning Commission, which was considering changing rigid ordinances against working out of the home. These ordinances referred generally to businesses; however, it could have been used against telecommuters as well.

Paul discovered that most of the people who were against changing the ordinance were sixty or older. When these people thought of home businesses, Edwards reasoned, they thought of services such as hair salons or mechanic shops, which increased traffic in the neighborhood (which is what the ordinance was supposed to prevent). They didn't know that the majority of home workers are white-collar employees who run clean businesses and telecommute. The only increased traffic would be over the phone lines, with possibly a slight rise in UPS and express-mail visits. Most of the people who spoke for changing the ordinance were in their thirties and forties, and either already had experience working from home or knew quite a few people who did.

A Compromise

Sometimes, no matter what you've said or done to show how telecommuting will help you, your boss, your department, and the company as a whole, the people upstairs will still shake their heads and turn your proposal down. Unfortunately, this attitude isn't rare. Some companies still subscribe to the eagle-eye periscope version of management: Keep your eye on them at all times.

But maybe your immediate supervisor is sympathetic to your desire to telecommute and wants to help you out. On occasion, you'll find a "guerrilla telecommuter," which is a person who very quietly works at home on an occasional basis. Sometimes a guerrilla telecommuter's colleagues will have no idea that their coworker is spending a day or so every week working from home. Neither will the top brass at the company.

If there are several guerrilla telecommuters at a company and then other employees decide they want to work from home occasionally, the cat might get out of the bag. The telecommuter aspirants may point to their covert role models as examples of how telecommuting can benefit the company. Of course, if the guerrillas don't want to be unmasked, you may have a power struggle on your hands if you choose to fight for the right to work from home.

Sometimes a company may have a few "guerrilla managers" scattered about. These supervisors may think that certain employees have both the temperament and job duties to work effectively at home. However, instead of approaching his or her higher-ups for approval, the manager instead approaches the employee, who may already have been trying to work up the courage to ask for permission to work at home part-time. The employee is thrilled, and together the two of them draw up specific goals and timetables that revolve around telecommuting. After it's clear that telecommuting has succeeded on this small scale, then, armed with facts and figures that telecommuting can definitely work within the company, the manager approaches his or her supervisors, who tend to eyeball everything with a look toward the bottom line.

In this case, it might be a good idea for the manager to let some of the other managers in the department know what's going on, especially if they and their employees have regular contact with the guerrilla telecommuter.

In conjunction with this preliminary bit of information gathering, the manager might feel out his or her higher-ups before letting them know that an employee is telecommuting. For example, he or she might bring the subject up with a supervisor in casual conversation in order to gauge the reactions. Or either you or your supervisor might arrange to place a brief news item in the company newsletter giving one positive statistic about telecommuting—perhaps about the increased productivity that customarily goes along with it.

What if Your Boss Says No?

Telecommuting consultant Gil Gordon suggests that people whose request to telecommute is denied should try to put themselves in their boss's shoes. "It's usually very clear from the employee's point of view why he or she wants to telecommute," he says. "What's not clear from the manager's point of view is what's in it for him or her and for the company." Unless you have an extremely benevolent manager who's not worried about that, you've got to look at it from the boss's perspective. Think about the ways in which telecommuting will help you do your job better, help you better service your clients, and help you stay with the organization. "I wouldn't necessarily use that as a threat," says Gordon, "but if you are not able to have that flexibility, you may not be able to stay in the job, and if you're a valued trusted employee, then you have some leverage."

The second step is to present telecommuting as a solution to your manager, not a problem. Says Gordon: "Don't say, 'I'd like to try telecommuting, how can we figure it out?' I think it's better to go in and say here's why and here's how. Take the time to do your homework and iron out the details." For instance, specify the number of days each week you're going to telecommute, how you're going to get your mail, what's going to happen with your telephone on the days you're working from home, and what's going to happen when somebody comes by your desk. Ask the "What if?" questions you know the boss is going to ask. Anticipate them and come up with the answers so the boss knows you've thought the idea through.

The third step is to be modest in your expectations in the beginning. "If you can get a commitment from your boss to let you work at home for as little as one day a week for a month or two in the beginning, that can be a big accomplishment," says Gordon. "And it's instrumental in demonstrating that you can do it. Sometimes managers who are faced with something different, even if they understand it, are fearful of committing to something with no end to it. Make it bite-sized and begin on a trial basis, and then you and your boss will reevaluate it at the end. If it makes sense, you'll continue with it. Then you're giving the manager an easy way to back out of it later." But your supervisor probably won't.

If your boss still won't let you telecommute, throw out this enticement: Offer to do the jobs that no one else in the office wants to do, as long as you can do them at home. For example, you might win over your boss by agreeing to be on call evenings or weekends, when no one else wants to work. It can get convoluted, but you can keep track of the number of hours you work during these times and then make up the rest of the time in the office during the week. Or you may be able to arrange with the company that your entire job is to be on call during off-hours; that way, you can have your days free. Be as creative as you can manage. The response you'll get from your boss may surprise you.

If you can, talk to a manager within your company who already manages some or all of his or her employees from afar. You might start by looking for a sales manager who supervises a far-flung group of representatives, each with his or her own territory, which may be a thousand miles away. What techniques does the manager use to stay in touch with employees? Is it necessary that they meet in person every so often? What problems arise? What are the benefits of having a remote work force? If the manager has no time to answer your questions, perhaps his or her secretary or assistant can help. But one thing is clear: The fact that there already is a successful telecommuting program in place in your company will help you make your case to work at home.

Typical Arguments Against Telecommuting

☐ *It's too expensive to implement.* Not necessarily. Not every employee who telecommutes needs a computer at home. And, most companies have a stockpile of old computers sitting around in the storeroom collecting dust. Equipping a telecommuter with one of these older computers costs nothing.

☐ *You can't trust your employees to work a full day if they're out of your sight.* Many telecommuting studies have indicated that the majority of employees not only work a full day but go well beyond what is expected of them. The issue of trust involved in telecommuting goes both ways: The employee who telecommutes trusts the supervisor that the arrangement will continue if everyone involved is satisfied, and the supervisor trusts that the telecommuter will be able to get his or her work done. This is one of the criticisms of mandatory telecommuting programs: They don't rest on that layer of trust. After working with an employee for a certain period of time, most supervisors are able to determine whether the worker would work well at home, so the element of trust develops.

☐ *Employees who telecommute are less likely to get promoted than their office-bound colleagues.* In some cases this has been true, so telecommuters must make an extra effort to stay in touch not only with his or her own manager and coworkers but also with supervisors in other departments and their employees. It may seem patently unfair, but extra effort is required at this stage of telecommuting, because many people are unsure how to deal with you. The good news is that your communication in these cases will usually be held to the minimum. You can focus on your goals and results by corresponding via e-mail, fax, and phone.

☐ *You'll end up losing productivity because telecommuters will just goof off.* Again, this is a matter of trust. Over and over again, employees and managers say they can't quite believe that a worker's productivity could jump that much—in some cases, up to 50 percent or more—simply because of telecommuting. As a telecommuter adjusts to working from home, productivity may dip a bit in the first week or two, but it doesn't take long for the figures to jump.

☐ *Everybody will want to telecommute, and then there will be no office staff left.* Even with mandatory telecommuting, companies will still need a support staff to carry on back in the office. Alvin Toffler predicted that as telecommuting continued to spread in the U.S. corporations, entire office buildings would become vacant and rush-hour traffic jams would cease to exist. But these things won't happen, even if 50 percent of American workers choose to telecommute part of the time.

Besides, not everyone wants to telecommute in the first place. Think about the people in your own office. Conduct a test: Who would be a good telecommuter, and who wouldn't last the week?

□ *Managers won't like it because they'll have to learn to manage in a different way.* In the past, managers have learned to manage their employees through a combination of trial and error and heavy reliance on the bookwork they did at business school. However, many managers were in for a shock in the 1980s, as they discovered that the old management styles didn't always take hold. For one thing, the influx of women and minorities forced managers to make at least some minor adjustments. Then came downsizing, and all hell broke loose as the old rules became dinosaurs and the new rules became "learn as you go."

So even though a manager may balk at the prospect of learning how to manage employees who are not right under his or her nose, given the dynamic patterns that many managers operate under today, he or she probably won't be the least bit flustered at your request. Instead, your manager may welcome it, because telecommuting actually shifts some of the supervisory burden to the employee. Keep this in mind if your boss turns you down.

PROFILE OF A TELECOMMUTER: EMILY BASSMAN

Emily Bassman is the director of virtual-office development at Pacific Bell. Her territory covers the whole state of

California. She works to promote telecommuting and the virtual office within the company to try to inform managers and employees about the advantages. "We already have an active telecommuting program," she says, "and what I'm trying to do is move it to a different level to get people to see that it's much more than just a flexible work option."

For instance, she cites a new fax-on-demand system designed to get information to employees as easily as possible, an online telecommuter user's manual, and an 800 number that people can call to ask questions about telecommuting—what you need to do it, whom to call, and what type of equipment you might need. Bassman says this is a good alternative to producing a printed manual.

Her aim in developing these resources is to inform people so they can decide whether or not telecommuting would work for them. But why go to all the bother when telecommuting is already big at the company? Bassman says Pacific Bell and its employees will benefit from her programs in a lot of different ways. "Technology has changed so much that it's feasible to help people to get offsite and then to keep in touch. It can increase effectiveness and productivity and enable our employees to be much closer to their customers, whether it's an external customer or internal client," she says.

Another of the benefits she cites, reduced real estate expenses, can only be reaped if a lot of people start to telecommute routinely. "Then you can reduce the amount of office space people are using," she says. "If people are telecommuting three days a week, obviously they don't need a dedicated office: they can share one instead."

The company does have some satellite offices set up and may elect to open more in the future. One team of salespeople has instituted a virtual office for every member, and they all share one work space back at the main office. They also have the use of satellite offices that are near their customers. In fact, says Bassman, a lot of these salespeople live near their customers. "It makes more sense for them to utilize satellite offices when they're in between meetings instead of coming all the way back to the main offices," she says. The satellite offices are small by necessity and are used only by one work group.

Bassman says Pacific Bell's technical and sales groups contain the employees who use telecommuting most. "And the tech groups really use it in a big way," she says. Almost every group at the company has some people who telecommute. They may not telecommute several times a week—in fact, some telecommute pretty infrequently—but they're still telecommuting. Most of the company's employees seem to like telecommuting and take advantage of it if they can.

Bassman works two to three days a week from home, mainly because it's her job to demonstrate that it can be done. "Some of the work I do I can do much better at my home office because it requires concentration. For instance, a lot of my work involves writing, thinking, and integrating information. My office is eighteen miles away from my house, and I work with a lot of other people, but we're basically a virtual team, since they don't work directly for me and are in other departments. We all get together once a month and talk about our issues," she says.

As for the genesis of telecommuting versus that of the virtual office, Bassman says that's no chicken-or-egg issue: "Telecommuting came first, and the virtual office came off of that because you need more sophisticated equipment for a virtual office," she says. "Telecommuting had to happen first on a less frequent basis in order for people even to begin to envision the possibility of being away from the office."

Before she began working as the director of virtual-office development, Bassman worked in human resources at

Pacific Bell, where part of her job was to set telecommuting policy. Her new position, to which she moved in 1993, is an extension of the earlier post.

She estimates that between 13 and 15 percent of all management employees at Pacific Bell telecommute part-time. Like many experts, she thinks telecommuting will become less of a separate issue and more a part of the whole corporate picture. "I think the idea of telecommuting is just going to disappear because people are just going to get used to the idea of working in all these different places," she says. "In fact, that's what's happening right now. When we conducted a survey of managers' attitudes toward telecommuting in 1989, there was one group who considered themselves to be telecommuters and another group who worked at home just as frequently who didn't label themselves telecommuters. They didn't think about it as a formalized work option; it was just something they did."

"What continually surprises me in terms of the growth of telecommuting is the enormous potential for people to improve their productivity and job satisfaction," she adds. "And that's what I do all day."

5

*Setting Up
Your Home Office*

=========================

*The office itself and most of our models for informa-
tion technology today are industrial models. The
notion of an office really is just a wholesale transposi-
tion of industrial processes. We process words in the
same way we process metal to put into a car. And
when you have a processing mentality, a place for processing, like an office, is essential. But the moment we
abandon that processing model and go to stranger and
newer models, then the idea of having a physical place
where you go and sit down and have a desk and a
stapler and all that becomes very quaint.*

—Paul Saffo, director at the Institute for the Future,
Menlo Park, California

In order for both the employee and the company to benefit from telecommuting, you need to be in a space where

---

you can maintain your focus on your job, which is first and foremost. In order to accomplish this, you'll need a quiet area in which to work, and you'll need to set aside time to work—you can't wash dishes or care for children when you're supposed to be working—and you'll need proper equipment, which depends on what you plan to do at home.

The software and hardware that make telecommuting easier get faster and easier to use every day, and new products are appearing on the market almost daily. If your employer has set you up with everything you need according to a well-worn, well-utilized telecommuting program, then you can skip to the next section—"Working From Your Car." If you're a pioneer telecommuter, however, you're on your own and will have to do your own homework. If you save for tele-commuting the kind of work that doesn't require a computer, just quiet and time, you can also skip to the next section.

Computerizing Your Home Office

If you plan to correspond with the office from home, at the very least you'll need a computer, an e-mail software package, and a second phone line so you can talk on the phone while you're on-line. A second phone line used strictly for business (it can be set up as a residential line to save costs) also facilitates bookkeeping and tax computation at the end of the year. If you are your company's first telecommuter and no other employee needs to send e-mail from remote locations, the corporate office will also have to hook up a separate phone line in order to receive your e-mail and send messages back to your home office.

Local Area Networks

If you can't wait until you get back to the office to get into your company's database, you'll need to be equipped with a remote LAN package to connect you to the network server back at the office. Depending on the package, you may be able to get into the files on your office computer's hard drive and even print out documents on the office laser printer, all from your home office.

ISDN

Integrated Services Digital Network (ISDN) technology will receive a lot of attention and generate a lot of new installations among telecommuters over the rest of the 1990s. ISDN is the fastest way to send digitized images over phone lines. It will facilitate videoconferencing and other instances where you need to send pictures from one location to another. However, at this time, this technology is still being developed, and there's a long way to go before the images are smooth and flawless. In order to get set up with ISDN, you'll need to sign up for special service with your phone company, and buy hardware that connects you to a LAN. Of course, you'll also require cameras and microphones on both ends. And that's just the beginning.

As CD-ROM and other technological marvels that seemed like science fiction only two years ago continue to become more commonplace, prices will tumble, and the technology will become faster and better. If you don't want to invest several thousand dollars in a soon-to-be inferior system, then wait until the technology improves. PCs will soon offer much higher power and speed in order to accommodate business applications that require 120 MHz and 150 MHz Pentium-class chips.

Desktop Conferencing Software

If you need the ability to view a file from a coworker's hard drive on your own screen while the two of you discuss it on the phone, or if he or she needs to be able to see a document from your home computer's hard drive, you'll need document conferencing software, which allows either user to send a document through the LAN network so that both users can view it and make notes on it at the same time. Some programs only allow two people to work together at a time; others allow three or more users to view a document and make changes.

Desktop conferencing programs include several different versions of ProShare by Intel. The basic version allows each person to make notes on the screen. An advanced version, called ProShare Premiere Edition, can also tap into a word processing or spreadsheet program that's running on one of the participants' computers. If you want to do more than just jot down notes—that is, if you want to actually institute changes to the document itself—these more advanced versions are better suited for you. Another plus is that even though only one person may have a copy of ProShare, the other can easily download it so that the two can work together.

System Differences

What happens when two remote users are working on two different computers, one a Windows-based IBM, and the other a Macintosh? No problem. A document conferencing system called Face to Face will allow participants to work together on documents even if their computers are not compatible.

The Universal In-Box

You've probably already started to see the advent of the all-in-one voice mail, fax, speakerphone, and e-mail unit. One wit has already referred to it as the "universal in-box." Indeed, it does make working from home easier, especially if you're short on space. Voice-recognition software can make this system as hands-free as you like. The only problem I can see with it is that when you return to the office, if you don't have a secretary to take your messages, you may wish you were back working in your home office.

Cellular Everything

Some devotees of the virtual office are already touting cellular and wireless fax, e-mail, and downloading capabilities even though their performance often leaves something to be desired. As with other high-tech devices, the day in the sun for these truly magical instruments of communication is still down the road. The bugs, which include lots of static and unexpected disconnects (usually at the most inopportune moments), are still being ironed out. With cellular modems, the faster the transmission speed, the more likely that mistakes will be made. In addition, data signals sent via cellular can be easily picked up by anyone who would be interested in your words. And encryption software for cellular data is a *long* way down the pike.

When the bugs are eliminated, however, you will be able to work out of a cabin in the middle of the woods—or somewhere on a beach. And unless your supervisor has access to videoconferencing devices, no one will be the wiser; your company will think you're at home writing those brilliant reports.

Eat at Big Boy

Even AT&T is getting into the act. In late 1994 the company began taking out full-page ads in the *Wall Street Journal* and other publications touting its new computer system, the Globalyst 360 TPC. The ad read: "Introducing the first PC&C for work-at-home. It's a speakerphone, a fast modem.

It's listening to voice mail while you're sending a fax. It's how to eat the Big Boy's lunch." IBM created an image of telecommuters comfortably working at home, calling their own shots, while the guys in the suits and ties are forty stories up, jockeying for position in unproductive power struggles.

Further down in the ad, AT&T explained how it designed the Globalyst: "We listened to what people like you said about how they work. And created a solution that works like an entire office. Complete with secretary."

Well, maybe not quite that. But the Globalyst does boast a separate combination speaker/microphone that's not built in to the computer, so that during a conference call you can relax on your home-office sofa and not be confined to your desk. The system also contains a built-in personal phone directory that works with Caller ID to match a number or a name, so you know whether it's your boss calling or the long-distance phone sales rep trying to get you to switch your service.

Getting By With Less

The easiest and most streamlined solution is simply to rely on a laptop computer and docking stations at both your home office and the regular office. This way, you take your all-purpose primary computer with you wherever you go and always know what's on your hard drive. If you don't have LAN capabilities that allow you to hook into the network at the office, you don't have to keep track of what files and programs are on which computer or carry around a bunch of copied floppy disks with you.

Here's how it works: You work on your laptop when you're at home. When you're working in the office, you hook your laptop into a docking station at your desk that provides access to the company's computer network. You can then download files and work at a capacity far greater than your laptop's hard drive RAM could support alone. Most docking stations also have additional ports allowing you to add a CD-ROM drive, speakers, and other external devices.

Because the price of a notebook can run several thousand dollars and a docking station at least a grand, your company may not be willing to provide you with this level of technology and may require you to rely on a notebook or a stationary desktop system. These computers will work fine, but your expansion and at-home capabilities may be a bit limited, especially if you are unable to hook into your office network.

Of course, you may need nothing more than a typewriter or paper and pencil if you use your work-at-home days to think, read, or write. And if you have to supply your own equipment and you're on a tight budget, this may have to suffice.

Some people decide to buy used computer equipment. However, you may be taking a big risk, especially if your office technical support staff cannot repair equipment that the company didn't purchase (or if your company is too small to have a tech staff). Hard drives crash and programs freeze up (usually when you're on deadline), and if you are one of those whose boss is averse to telecommuting, then you might as well resign yourself to a long commute Monday through Friday if such problems leave you unable to do your job. So if you can't buy new equipment, try to get used equipment with a warranty. I've found that buying used computer equipment from an independent service technician who regularly installs new corporate systems and buys back the old ones will give you your best value. Ask for a service warranty and the ability to call in for help with technical problems.

The Gartner Group, a consulting firm in Stamford, Connecticut, claims that it costs a company from $2,000 to

$4,000 to set up a telecommuter with all the equipment he or she needs to work from home. The firm estimates monthly work-related telephone bills at between $100 and $200 a month. Although this is another company expense, most firms have a dedicated long-distance WATS line or another system that provides deep discounts for heavy usage. The increased productivity the company gets from the employee more than offsets the increased phone cost.

Moving Data Around

A variety of software programs exist to help move data back and forth between home office and corporate office and to facilitate the movement of information from one workstation to another.

A company named Sigma Imaging Systems has produced a software package, called OmniDesk Home Workstation, that facilitates image transfers. Employees who are working from home can easily receive document images, work with and alter them, and then easily send them back to the office. The software's main benefit is speed. Many modems send and receive images at a snail's pace. This software package zooms the images along from office mainframe to home laptop or desktop at high speed, so you'll never notice the slowdown that occurs with many image transference programs.

Protecting Your Investment

You should definitely buy a surge protector for your computer, fax, copy machine, and other electronic equipment. Electrical power supplies in private homes are often unpredictable, and the power can spike—that is, suddenly increase. Without a surge protector to absorb that excess power, the surplus electricity can enter your electrical equipment, which may destroy all the inner components and render your system useless.

You'll also want to be sure that you don't have your office located in a room that serves as the point of entry for your electrical service. Again, surges are a factor, and they can quickly fry your computer to a crisp, although you wouldn't notice it until you tried to turn it on and nothing happened.

Working From Your Car

In recent years more and more employees have been using their cars as a part-time office base, whether intentionally or not. A professional resource firm in Boston, the Yankee Group, reports that currently 6 million Americans work from their cars most of the time, and millions more use their automobiles as a temporary base at least some of the time. Both of these figures will increase by 25 percent in the next five years, the Yankee Group estimates. Most of these vehicles—more than 90 percent—also double as the family vehicle. If you've just dropped your daughter off at day care, and she left her opened lunchbox or her toys behind on the back seat, and you have to pick up one of the major shareholders at the airport in fifteen minutes, you're going to have trouble.

In the February 22, 1995, issue of the *Wall Street Journal*, L. B. Gschwandtner, editor of *Personal Selling Power* magazine, offered a great picture of the employee who works from a car that doubles as Mom's Taxi: "We're like turtles, toting the paraphernalia of multiple roles around on our backs." Telecommuters can have this problem, especially if documents and equipment have to be regularly shuffled around from home office to corporate office.

To remedy this problem and to make the vehicle look as

corporate as possible (at least from the outside), some people rely on tinted windows. Others have a vinyl sheet or blanket they throw over any offending materials that have been inadvertently left in the back seat. Still others relegate any junk to a trunk that locks. There are special car organizers that can be secured to the floor with Velcro, which keeps it from sliding around and allows you to move it in an instant when a corporate VIP is seen approaching your car. If you drive a conversion van, you can make the back your living and/or working space and create a divider between the back and the front, or driving, area. Some people totally outfit their vans with computer, fax, printer, files, and cellular phone. Do that and you'll be a *real* telecommuter.

Getting Technical Help

Another problem you may run into whenever you work at home is the lack of an on-site technical support team. You can call them at the main office, of course, but you may find it difficult to get any help when you can't tell them how much memory is left on your hard drive or how many error messages appear when you run your config.sys program.

Software specifically designed to troubleshoot computer problems can make your life a bit easier. You can get a program called WinSleuth Gold that provides you with a detailed analysis of your hardware. You can then call the tech support department back at the office in order to get some idea of why your screen has frozen up. Another good program, System Info Plus, is a shareware program that analyzes your hardware system and performs a number of tests to further winnow down the list of possible problems.

But the best choice may simply be to use a laptop. Laptops are portable and flexible, can do whatever a desktop-bound computer can do, and can plug into the company's mainframe no matter where its user is located. Link Resources, the New York consulting firm, says 16 percent of all computers used at home are laptops, and that figure will continue to grow as these machines become more powerful.

Another advantage of a laptop is that it's portable inside your house. If you need a break from your home office, you can take your computer into the living room, the bedroom, even outside. And laptops don't take up a lot of room, an important consideration if your home office is by necessity tiny. Because of these space considerations, you may need to consolidate other pieces of office equipment as well. For example, you can buy a machine that combines phone, answering machine, fax, copy machine, and computer all in one.

If you need help occasionally with your high-tech equipment, you don't have to turn to the technical support department within your company—if indeed, it exists. Office supply companies and computer manufacturers often provide technical assistance. You may have to sign up in advance and provide proof of purchase, and sometimes a fee is incurred, but you can't beat this kind of personalized assistance, especially early on, when your boss isn't yet 100 percent sold on your telecommuting arrangement and you don't want to jeopardize it.

Certain companies have contracted with Kinko's to use the national chain's copy centers as telework centers. Kinko's outlets not only provide copiers, fax machines, computer rentals and laptop ports, but also make it possible to set up videoconferences. Some even offer the use of private conference rooms for telecommuters who need an outside base. In fact, Kinko's is promoting its centers with these capabilities as virtual branch offices for telecommuters who need to perch there.

Telecommuting Snapshot

In Nevada City, California, Gary and Deborah Aufdenspring put a "telecommuting house" on the market to capitalize on the future work revolution. The couple put all the information about the home on a computer floppy disk, complete with typical sounds that can be heard on the property, (chirping birds, crickets, etc.). They geared their sales pitch to telecommuters by including information about mail and express mail deliveries, a map of a nearby telecommuting center, and a floor plan of the home office, which displays phone jacks, electrical outlets, and plenty of built-in shelves. Information on local zoning—the area, fortunately, boasts a liberal home-office ordinance—is also included.

The Aufdensprings' program, called "Telecommuting House for Sale," takes up 2 megabytes of hard-drive space and is available through both America Online and Apple eWorld. If you want to see what the ideal house for telecommuters looks like, you can download from the new files area of the Hypercard Forum or contact Gary Aufdenspring, PO Box 1128, Nevada City CA 95959-1128, or call 916-477-1421. As of late winter 1995, the house, which comes with thirty-eight acres, was still available.

Furniture

If you've been in any of the chain office supply stores, you've undoubtedly seen their all-in-one desk consoles and workstations, which are probably better than anything you've worked with in your regular office. But before you start drooling and whipping out your credit card in a bit of vengeance fantasy—"I'm going to have an office that's even nicer than my boss's"—carefully consider what you need and how you're going to work at home. Do you need a desk that fits in a compact space? Several tables where you can spread out papers, books, and other research materials? Do you need lots of storage space, or will your equipment needs at home be minimal? You'll need to focus carefully on these questions if the company isn't paying for your office equipment.

However, at least one major manufacturer has a furniture line geared specifically toward the home-office worker. In the summer of 1994, Crate and Barrel, the nationwide furniture and houseware retail chain, introduced a new line of furniture designed to accommodate the needs of telecommuters and small-business owners who work from a home office. Some pieces feature table wings that easily fold out of sight when you're through working and a built-in document holder that tilts to the angle that's most comfortable for you. Crate and Barrel also offers a complete home-office furniture system, complete with desk, bookcases, and drawers. Each piece of furniture is designed to deal with the wormlike tangles of power cords that regularly get tangled underfoot. (It's not a good thing to be kicking your feet underneath your desk while taping an interview and suddenly dislodge the power cord to the tape recorder.)

Don't expect the same type of prices on this furniture that you see all the time at warehouse office supply stores. This furniture is made of solid cherry, not particle board. A simple writing desk will be priced at $599. A complete office setup will go for about $2,500. However, with the success of Crate and Barrel's marketing drive, the warehouse stores can't be far behind, and they'll surely offer lower prices. At the same time Crate and Barrel was introducing its home-office furniture line, the warehouse chain Office Depot was planning to bring out a line of home-office furniture a few months hence. Who knows? Soon people who work from home may be able to shop at a store called Home Office Depot.

AT&T is still perfecting its version of the picturephone, which has been touted as the next big thing since "The Jetsons" was airing in prime time. Unlike the earlier, crude models, this new picturephone can deliver and receive clear, full-motion images across standard telephone lines for no additional cost. However, the model needs some additional work before it is introduced to the public on a mass scale, which should happen soon simply because the demand is there.

Safety Concerns at Your Home Office

Many companies with formal telecommuting policies are very specific about the equipment they require telecommuters to have in and around their home offices. Even though the employee would be liable for damage to equipment in case of a fire, burglary, or accident, it benefits everyone if a telecommuter's home office is as professional as possible. That means maintaining the same amount of attention to detail that the company pays at the corporate headquarters. Bell Atlantic, for example, spells out in its telecommuting guidelines that any employee who works from home must have a fire extinguisher, smoke detector, fire-escape plan, and first-aid kit. The company also requires telecommuters to have three-wire cords and plugs on all motor-driven electronic equipment with metal housings; to use grounding adapters; and not to overload outlets. It even has a section on chairs, ostensibly to cut down on back-pain complaints that may be caused by a substandard office chair in the home. Employees must inspect chairs to make sure the tension is set correctly and even check the casters and fabric to ensure that they're in good condition. The guidelines also instruct telecommuting employees to situate desks, tables, and chairs so they don't block exits and entrances, to close cabinet drawers when they're not in use, and to store heavier material in the lower drawers.

All these rules are necessary in order to comply with OSHA (Occupational Safety and Health Administration) regulations that specify that employers must make sure their work spaces are "free from recognized hazards that cause, or are likely to cause, death or serious injury or harm." Larger companies will often send out a member of their facilities maintenance or occupational health team to a telecommuter's home to inspect the office and make sure it is in compliance with federal occupational safety standards. As you can see, to meet these standards you may be forced to fill a shopping cart with fire extinguishers, first-aid kits, and the like.

Occupational safety is a matter of common sense. But the question that naturally arises is: Does the company pay this much attention to the furniture back at the corporate office? Companies may emphasize safety in the home office to cut down on health insurance claims arising from negligence on the part of the employee, but their concern does seem excessive at times. My suggestion is find furniture that works and is comfortable and then use it.

Who Should Pay for the Equipment?

The majority of companies either supply telecommuting employees with surplus equipment and pay for an additional business phone line or buy new equipment outright.

Some companies—most notably the public utilities—tend to make the employee pay for a computer, modem, fax machine, and copier. They usually do offer to pay for the phone line.

A new issue in the world of telecommuting is whether or not employees should be reimbursed for the "rental" of their home by their employer. After all, the employer is "renting" the home-office space for the employee and, it can feasibly be argued, should pay for it. But then you get into sticky tax laws concerning employee income, the home-office deduction, and so forth. As more people begin to telecommute and employees learn that their employer should pay them for renting part of their space, the issue of rental reimbursement will come to the forefront.

Comfort and Convenience

Back at the office, if you felt physically uncomfortable in your work space, the only choice you had was to grin and bear it—unless you were the boss. Thankfully, things are different in your home office. In fact, besides the elimination of the commute, the thing you may be most looking forward to about working from home is the fact that you'll have your own office, designed to be most conducive to your work habits.

It's important that it be in a separate room if possible. Not only is this required if you decide to deduct the cost of a home office from your taxes, but it also sends a message to yourself, your family, and your friends: "This is a work space; when I'm in here and the door is closed, it means I'm busy working." Conversely, it also means that you can leave the office when the day is over and shift into your off-hours life. One thing about working at home is that work is always near, making it very hard to ignore. That's one of the few things that can be said in favor of working in a regular office: Unless your job commonly requires you to bring work home, you leave it behind at quitting time. It's important that you set up the same arrangement at home.

I've always worked from home, and though I've had a separate room for an office several times, more generally I've set up my desk and computer in a spare alcove with no door. Not only does it make this arrangement make it hard to leave work behind, but books, papers, and other work materials have the uncanny ability to overflow into other areas of the house. Usually if I want to eat at the kitchen table, I have to transfer piles of papers, books, and bills to the sofa. Then, when I want to sit on the sofa . . . well, you get the idea.

So get a separate office.

It's also important that the space you choose for your home office be free of interruptions and distractions. If you have room on the quiet side of the house, set up your office there. If there's a television in the room, get it out. You don't want to have even the tiniest temptation to wonder what Oprah and Geraldo are up to when your clock reads 3:13, so the best thing to do is to remove the set from the room before you ever begin to work there.

PROFILE OF A TELECOMMUTER: DAVID HALL

In the May 23, 1994 issue of *Forbes*, writer R. Lee Sullivan profiled David Hall, a Compaq salesman, who stayed at the company as one of 224 survivors after 135 colleagues were laid off. An increase in productivity was expected of the survivors. New sales quotas were set to double revenues, and the company gave each salesperson the equipment to accomplish these goals.

David Hall works out of a spare bedroom in his Houston

home. He uses a Compaq LTE Lite 486 notebook computer with a 200-megabyte hard drive. At home he plugs the notebook into a docking bay that hooks into a color monitor, tape backup drive, and laser printer. He also works with a machine that combines fax and copier capabilities, a cellular phone, two outside phone lines, and some office furniture. Each day he plugs into the Compaq server network back at the office. The network contains an enormous database that updates Hall on to-date and monthly sales figures for his department, provides information about contacts that his colleagues have made, and contains press releases and other marketing materials that he may need to draw on in order to close a sale.

Before the company and department were drastically overhauled, these pieces of information were contained on separate networks, which made them time-consuming and difficult to find. Now everything is contained on one server that any employee anywhere in or outside the office can log on to, which leaves more time for dealing with customers. Hall can also hook into Compaq's main server network on the road with a cellular phone or a standard phone jack.

Hall says the major advantage of his setup is portability. "We don't have to carry around overhead projectors and transparencies," he told *Forbes.* In addition, he doesn't have to lug around a briefcase full of different brochures or wait until he gets back to the office to send a client a brochure on a particular product. Instead, he prints a brochure in a client's office on his laser printer. Ann Bacon, a sales rep at Farmland Foods in Kansas City, works on a system similar to David Hall's—a system that Compaq sold to the meat-packing company. "You can see their eyes light up when we access the database right from [the client's] office," says Bacon.

Animals and Your Home Office

You may not have considered the issue of having a cat or dog hang out with you while you work, but if you are a pet owner, believe me, the issue will come up.

Perhaps you'll deal with it simply. Maybe the cat has already thrown up once in the printer or the dog has tried to jump up on your lap and in the effort knocked your coffee into the computer keyboard. So from simple experience, you've learned to close the door to keep out not only your kids and neighbors but also your pets.

For the rest of you, however, it'll be a little different. Picture this scenario: You're stuck at home working, and although you enjoy the total lack of interruptions from your officemates, you still feel a bit lonely. You don't want human company, but a living breathing *something* in the room might be nice, especially if it does nothing more than sleep.

I've always had at least one of my three cats work by my side when I'm sitting at the computer or sitting on the sofa writing longhand. It helps me keep my rhythm. Cats are usually content not to have your full attention as long as you're not interacting with another human. When you're on the phone, therefore, they might cause trouble—say, walk on the keyboard before you've had a chance to save that important report you've worked on all morning, or step on the phone and disconnect you. Of course, these are all accidents, but they do happen from time to time. Still, I am willing to risk them. I spend a lot of my time working by myself, whether I'm talking on the phone or not, and I find cats the perfect companions.

Of course, there are drawbacks. When I take in my computer to be serviced once a year, my technician always asks if a mouse has been living in there. He invariably pulls out big clumps of gray fur from around the hard drive—which is enclosed, thank goodness. Cats and dogs can be insistent. Sometimes when I sit on the sofa and talk on the cordless, one of my cats will loudly voice her unhappiness that I have stopped petting her. Customers usually ask if I have a baby; I say, no, I have a cat. Although some people may find this explanation awkward and not conducive to conveying a professional image, something like this can help break the ice if you're talking to someone with whom you're not familiar.

Zoning Regulations

One of the things you must consider is whether working from your home is against local zoning ordinances. Although the laws often list a broad range of businesses that cannot be run from a private home, many of these ordinances were enacted decades ago, when the majority of people working from home were in service businesses that brought a steady stream of traffic into the neighborhood.

Most telecommuters today just keep quiet about working from home. In most cases, it's impossible to know who's home during the day and who's not, especially in quiet suburban areas. Even if there is a rule against doing commerce at home (which is how some of the laws phrase it), most people will look the other way if they know a neighbor is breaking the law and working from home. They may even welcome it, because it means that there's someone around who can notice suspicious behavior or receive special deliveries.

However, certain people always need to stir things up. Even if you're not bothering anyone by working at home a couple of days a week, a neighbor can haul you before the local authorities and have you cited for breaking the law. You'll have to prove that you're not in violation. Many outdated home-office ordinances are changed when a telecommuter or home-based entrepreneur who provides tax revenue and security to the town challenges the laws. When this happens in smaller communities, it usually makes news, with neighbors lining up behind one or the other.

Whatever the law in your town says about working at home, chances are it won't affect you either way. As more and more people work at home, the laws will cease to be an issue. But there's still a long way to go. Home-office experts Paul and Sarah Edwards claim that only one out of five areas of the country can truly be regarded as friendly to people who work out of their homes.

Tax Regulations

Once upon a time—say, back in the 1970s—home-office tax deductions were plentiful. Back then, working from home usually meant bringing work home from the office. When an employee had to bone up, polish an important presentation, or meet a deadline that was written in stone, he or she brought the work home. It was usually done in a corner of the sewing room or on part of the dining room table.

That corner of the sewing room or portion of the dining room table was typically written off as a business expense. Nowadays if you do that, you might as well attach little red flags to your tax return. The IRS is extremely suspicious of home-office deductions, whether you have your own business at home or not. Most employees' office expenses don't add up to much, so they usually don't take the deduction. Other telecommuting employees aren't even aware that they can claim such expenses, including depreciation on the computer, fax machine, and other electronic equipment they use in their home offices—that is, if they bought the machines themselves. If your employer buys them for you, then the company gets the write-off.

You can, however, deduct part of your housing expenses if your home office meets one of three important criteria set down by the IRS to determine whether it is a bona fide business expense. Two of these criteria probably don't apply to you; they're used more often to determine the eligibility of a person who is running a business out of a home office.

☐ Your home office should be a place where clients, customers, and colleagues meet on a regular basis.

☐ You should be conducting business in your home office more than at the corporate office, and you shouldn't be using it as a kids' playroom or a laundry room when you're not working. The space has to be used for your business alone. The IRS asks if the home office is the principal place of business, which means that if you're telecommuting less than half the time, you probably can't take the deduction.

☐ If your home office is located in a separate building, even if you work fewer than three days at home, it's likely that all costs you incur in maintaining that separate building are deductible, including the equipment you use while there.

Of course, there are instances that may diverge from these three criteria. If you're in doubt, contact either your accountant or the IRS directly. If you'd like more information, contact the IRS to get a free copy of Publication Number 587: *Business Use of Your Home.*

If you choose to take the deduction, you have to fill out a separate form to attach to your return, Form 8829. Auditors are tougher on people who maintain home offices for any purpose, so the mere fact that you're filing the form will be the equivalent of waving a red flag in front of a bull. This explains why so many people don't bother to take the deduction at all, even if they qualify. People who work at home in their own small businesses easily pass the test for deducting the cost of the office space, so the IRS usually waves them on by. But telecommuters aren't so lucky. They are receiving a regular salary, and that steady paycheck signifies that they're probably not conducting all of their work from the home office. If you also run a small business on the side, your return will come under more scrutiny if you take the home-office deduction, because you'll have to verify with figures and logs that you spent most of your time working at home or made most of your money in the home office in order to justify the write-offs.

The wisest course is to confer with your accountant or other tax professional before you do anything. Examine all the pros and cons before you decide to take the write-off. And remember: If one area of your tax return catches the eye of an auditor, the rest of your return won't escape notice, either.

The tax aspects of working at home become even more confusing if your company is located in one state and you live in another. You and/or your employer may be liable for additional income tax in your home state. Most companies bypass this requirement, even if they're aware of it, by having their telecommuting employees work at home less than 50 percent of the time or by not informing that state government about the situation. Some people feel this double taxation is patently unfair. As more people begin to telecommute from one state to another and as state revenue offices start to scrounge around for more obscure sources of money, you can expect this issue to heat up.

Liability

If your company has a formal telecommuting policy in place and has had its lawyers go over it with a fine-toothed comb, you may have to sign a waiver agreeing that any personal injury, damage, or loss that occurs in your home office is not the company's fault. The reason? Your company is clearly liable should anything happen on its own property, but whatever happens in your home office is out of its control. Because of this, it's a good idea for you to check with your insurance company about the possibility of expanding your homeowners' policy to cover things such as damaged computer equipment or injuries that occur in your home office. Your company is not liable in such cases, so you may have to add provisions that cover the contingencies of having a home office. In fact, some experts believe that no one except you should use your home office, or even visit you in it, to limit your liability. Besides, your employer may insist that you meet with any clients or potential customers at its main headquarters, in part because of their need to maintain a corporate image.

The Inspection

It's possible that before you start telecommuting, your employer will want to inspect your home office to make sure it's up to snuff. At the City of Los Angeles, says Susan Herman of the telecommunications department, all telecommuting employees have to sign an agreement allowing a manager to inspect their home offices to make sure that the chosen space is suitable and that worker's compensation issues are properly addressed (for instance, are there wires hanging all over the place?). He or she will also inspect your phone system so the main office may deal with your phone calls, either with voice mail or call forwarding. Your work area and electrical service will also be checked to make sure that surges will be infrequent. After all, if the company is supplying the computer, it won't be pleased if an electrical jolt at your house fries the innards.

Herman says her main task is to reallocate resources. "We've defined telecommuting as bringing the work to the worker instead of the worker to the work," she says. "If your job can be done with a yellow pad and paper, you don't need to have a PC there. I have changed the allocation of desktop computer systems for some employees to laptops to allow for the flexibility of telecommuting. But the nature of an employee's work basically doesn't change. Somebody who wasn't using a computer before isn't suddenly going to start to use one."

PROFILE OF A TELECOMMUTER: JUDY LINDEN

Judy Linden, a book editor in New York, started telecommuting before it was fashionable, back in 1985. Today she works as executive editor at The Philip Lief Group, a book packager.

When her daughter was born in October 1984, she had been working as a senior acquisitions editor at G. P. Putnam's since 1978. While she was on maternity leave, she tried to find someone to look after her daughter so she could go back to work full-time, but she couldn't find anybody. On the day she was supposed to return to work, she went into the office and told the publisher she couldn't find a babysitter. "My boss was incredibly understanding and suggested I start working three days a week from home and two days a week in the office. And so I did," she says. "I continued that until my second child was three, and then I started working three days a week in the office."

During these early years, Linden didn't sit at a desk for eight hours a day when she was working at home. Instead, she read book proposals, edited manuscripts, and made business calls when the kids were napping or playing by themselves. She conducted her daily business and managed to fit in a lot of work over the course of a day. There were other working mothers at Putnam's who would work four days in the office and spend Fridays at home.

When she left Putnam's to work for the Philip Lief Group in 1992, Linden's reputation preceded her. "Philip and I agreed to keep my arrangement since I've always carried a full load." She says that doing a full-time job in three days a week has made her incredibly focused. She even was promoted to vice president and executive editor at Putnam's while she was telecommuting.

On the days that she works from home, publishers, writers, and coworkers frequently call her at home, but she doesn't have a separate phone line for business. She does have a study, but it's not hers alone, nor does she spend all of working-at-home time there. "It's the place where I hole up when I need to hole up," she says. "I may have some personal things going on at the same time I'm working at home, but I'm still able to work. I'm not interested in working at home five days a week, because I've always enjoyed Manhattan and having contact with other people in an office environment. Publishing is such a who-knows-what's-going-on kind of business that it's important for me to maintain my presence."

Linden says if you want to telecommute you should ask, even if you think it's impossible. "More and more people are working this way, even in industries where it was once considered impossible. I see doors are opening.

"The bottom line is that you probably give 140 percent as opposed to 100 percent because you value your arrangement and you want it to continue into the future. That's how you need to look at it," she says. "When I'm at the office, I try to do in three days what others may do in five. Here I also have more support. I have an assistant, copy machines, reference materials, and so on. Since I don't have these things at home, I take advantage of all I have here. I know what I have to do and when I have to do it, and I plot my days along those lines."

Unlike other telecommuters, Linden had never used a computer at home until recently. "When I was at Putnam's, it wasn't a problem because they were computerized and I had a full-time assistant," she says. "Besides, I always did my editing directly on the manuscript instead of on a computer, so I never really needed a computer. Now it's different, and I have a computer I can use at home." There are other employees at Philip Lief who work at home occasionally, particularly when they need to edit manuscripts, and everyone in her office agrees that certain tasks are better done from home.

Linden says that working from home suits certain people and not others. "For me it's second nature. I've done it now for ten years. Working at home has made me better organized, more productive, more focused, and more serious about my career. It may seem like something new and different, but once you adjust, it become easy."

She does say that she doesn't spend all of her time at home working. "I'm not plugged in all the time," she says. "When my kids come home from school it's nice to just tune out for awhile. I wouldn't have such a balanced life if I had to commute into the city five days a week. At some point I might do that, but while my kids are still young I want to be around for them. I feel I have the best of both worlds."

Telecommuting Snapshot

More than 50 percent of telecommuters use computers at home, and 10 percent use fax machines in their home offices.

Twenty-six percent of telecommuters use more than one phone line at home, but no more than 10 percent use business service lines. Business lines are more expensive, and there's no need for telecommuters to list a business name because most incoming calls will be forwarded from the main office.

As for calling services, approximately 18 percent of telecommuters use call forwarding, 38 percent use call waiting, and 10 percent use three-way calling.

6

Planning Your Day

You've done it. You're officially a telecommuter. Now what are you going to do? How will you structure your days? It all looked good on paper, but here's the moment of truth: You're telecommuting, and you don't have to get up and go anywhere. You'll have to motivate yourself. How do you start?

By setting goals.

Setting Your Goals

For many of us, the only way we know we're getting anywhere is if we set regular goals and then reach them before proceeding to the next. Telecommuting is no different.

The goals you set depend on the details you've worked out with your boss in advance. Out of necessity, some of these goals are going to be intangible ones. For instance, you may set a goal to write five letters to clients and call ten accounts on the phone on a particular day when you're working from home. These are tangible goals, and probably the ones foremost in your mind.

But somewhere in the back of your mind you think telecommuting will enable you to slow down your pace and spend more time with your family. These goals are intangible and can be measured only when you look back and compare your new, calm lifestyle with the chaos-induced frenzy that seemed like second nature to you before you began telecommuting.

Undoubtedly you'll have your own specific goals—both tangible and intangible—that you're interested in accomplishing during your time off. But you can use the following checklist as a guideline to start setting goals before you begin to telecommute. Keep in mind that some won't apply to you at all.

In your notebook, write the answers to the following questions:

- *Quantitative goals:* What do you want to accomplish by telecommuting? For instance, if you want to increase your productivity by 20 percent on the days you work from home, how does that apply to the kind of work you do? Twenty percent more phone calls? Letters? The number of report pages that you are able to write?

- *Qualitative goals:* If you desire a life that's more balanced between work and family, how will you be able to measure this?

- *After you've been telecommuting for about a year, what's next?* Do you think you'll be happy continuing in this vein, or would you like to work at home more or less of the time? Although it's difficult to envision how your life will change until you start to telecommute, it's still crucial to plan for how you're going to follow through.

□ *How do you see yourself doing things differently—in both your personal and professional life—once you start to work from home?*

It's difficult to know exactly how telecommuting will change your life until you start. But if you plan your telecommuting lifestyle carefully, you will have a somewhat clearer picture of how you're going to spend your time. In your notebook, write down your thoughts and actions to the following questions so that you are prepared for the unexpected. Then, once you start telecommuting and the unexpected arises, you can refer back to these answers in order to compare your fantasies with the reality and adjust your at-home work routine accordingly.

□ What are some of the expectations you have about working from home?

□ Are you prepared to switch gears if telecommuting starts to disappoint you, even in the slightest? How will you do it?

□ What external motivations will you set up to keep you going?

□ How will you maintain contact with the office?

□ What will you do if you or your boss decides you have to stop telecommuting?

□ Write down a schedule of your perfect telecommuting day.

Telecommuting is probably only the beginning of what will eventually be a much larger change in your life, one that you may only have dim thoughts of at this point. For example, what will happen once you start cutting down on your commute and start turning to your own neighborhood more for the things you need? As Susan Herman of the City of Los Angeles found out, "[telecommuters] were using the family vehicles in ways that consolidated their trips and were using community businesses in ways they had never done before, which added a whole new dimension to the quality of community life."

Once you start telecommuting, there's a good chance you'll have more leeway in how your run your life, where you choose to live, and how your community grows and thrives. If you're only one of a number of telecommuters in your town, just think about how the quality of life in your area will change.

Tracking Your Progress

It's pretty difficult to know in advance how quickly you'll progress when you first start to telecommute. But if you, with the help of your supervisor and coworkers, draw up a plan in advance and match yourself up against it every week or month, you'll have a rough guide to follow and to tinker with as you proceed.

If you're like me and tend to drastically underestimate the amount of time it will take you to accomplish a certain task, do yourself a favor: Deliberately overestimate the amount of time you think it will take you to complete a project at home. Then, if it takes less time than you think, you'll be pleasantly surprised. One of your aims when you work from home should be to find your natural rhythm of working. Frequently, the frenzied pace at which we are accustomed to handling the piles of work tends to obscure the depths we can reach. If you're the type who enjoys checking items off your priority list more than doing the actual tasks themselves, look to telecommuting as a way to begin enjoying work for its own sake rather than a way to earn a gold star on some amorphous chart. If you're telecommuting, your productivity will undoubtedly increase anyway; just try to start looking at your work in a different way.

If you're in the category of overachievers, it might be worth your while not to formally track your progress and instead to luxuriate in the task itself, with no thought of whether or not you're keeping up. This method is bound to make you uneasy at first. But I guarantee that if you work this way for a long enough period of time, you'll look back and marvel at the quality—and quantity—of the work you were able to produce. If you return to the old way of doing things, at least you'll look upon work with a different eye.

Telecommuting will force managers to adjust their styles of management. Rather than evaluating an employee's performance based on attendance, they'll have to look purely at the results. Janet Anderson, the director of the Midwest Institute for Telecommuting Education, put it this way in the institute's *Telecommuting Implementation Manual:* "Results of the work are all that can be observed and all that really matter. If, for example, two computer programmers are assigned the same problem to resolve, and one sits at a computer terminal trying out different solutions while the other goes for a walk to think about it—does it make a difference what their work methods are if they both determine the answer?"

Of course, this makes perfect sense, but it also runs counter to how most managers—and most employees—have been trained. One benefit of telecommuting is that if your agreement with a boss depends primarily on results and not on sitting at a desk—either in the corporate office or at your own home office—eight hours a day, you can work when you tend to work best. Very few people report that their peak hours fall between 9 in the morning and 5 in the afternoon. On the contrary, some people work best at 5 in the morning, while others aren't able to think clearly until the sun goes down. If results are the sole determinant of your job performance, and you don't have to take a lot of calls at home, and your family agrees, you may be able to work for concentrated periods of time when you're at your mental peak.

Getting—and Staying—Professional

Sometimes it may seem difficult to maintain a professional image while you're working at home, maybe in comfortable clothes, perhaps even in your pajamas. For this reason, many telecommuters choose to stick to a regular schedule and even get dressed in the clothes they'd ordinarily wear to the office. Here are three suggestions you can implement to build that attitude of professionalism while working at home.

1. *Maintain a separate phone line for business calls.* Have one line and just use it in your office; don't run extension phones off of it into other areas of the house. Only you should answer the phone. Don't have your kids answer if you're off in another corner of the house for a minute. Don't even have your spouse answer. The phone should only be used for business purposes.

2. *Talk with your supervisor several times each day.* Granted, the communication is going to differ from the conversations you have when you're in the office, but it's going to be more focused and less chatty, which will add to your productivity. When you're out of the office, you sometimes miss out on the nuances that can turn the course of a project slightly. If you keep in touch with your supervisor as well as some of your coworkers regularly, you can keep up with most of these developments.

3. *Treat the days you're working from home as your own.*
Take charge and let your independence motivate you to be
in the office at a set time each day and accomplish what
you set out to do. Not only does this approach mean that
you'll get a lot done, but you may start to think about running your own business. Then you'll be working from home
all the time instead of just a couple of days a week.

Going Beyond What Is Expected

Even though you may be working at home in your pajamas,
it's important that you maintain the aura of responsibility
when it comes to your job duties. You'll need to cultivate a
feeling of trust and accountability with all your coworkers,
your boss, and your customers as well. I should warn you
now that if anyone feels that you are shirking your responsibilities, starting to disregard deadlines, or letting things go
until the last minute, the critics back at the office will be
all over you in a second. They may feel as though you're
getting away with something by working at home. So it's
doubly important that you meet your deadlines and go
beyond what's expected of you in order not to undermine
the future of telecommuting at your company. Anyone who
chooses to be a pioneer in any field, not just telecommuting, will need to work twice as hard in order to get the
same praise accorded those who follow the status quo.
However, this burden shouldn't last forever; once your colleagues know you're still doing your job, their scrutiny
should decrease.

However, one problem inherent with telecommuting is
that it's easy to do too much, either because you seek to
quash the critics' doubts or simply because you get carried
away. Says Jack Robertson of Pacific Bell: "It's a good thing

to have your work with you all the time, and it's a bad thing to have your work with you all the time. Frequently, I'll say I'm going to do just one more thing, just one more thing, and if I start at 6 in the morning, the next thing I know I look up and it's 9 at night. Where did the day go? It's very easy to become a workaholic. You need to set some kind of parameters for yourself. Yes, the work is there, but you should recognize that it's still going to be there tomorrow."

People who work at home not only tend to work more hours than their office counterparts but also are usually able to work for several hours at a stretch without interruption, which would be impossible in most office settings. If the company allows it, one of the biggest benefits of working from home is that you can work during those times of the day or night when you are most productive. If you're a night owl, you can work into the wee hours; if your mind is clearest first thing in the morning, then you can jump right in at the crack of dawn.

This may not be possible for every telecommuter, but frequently you can schedule individual projects for those times of the day when you are at your best.

Should You Get Dressed?

Some people look forward to working at home because they can wear any clothes they want, even their pajamas, and don't have to spend half an hour or more each morning making themselves presentable for the office. Just think of the time you'll save! However, an awful lot of people out there equate wearing pajamas with lolling around the house on a lazy Saturday afternoon. They think their productivity will suffer, not thrive.

If you're one of these people, you just may have to fool yourself and make believe that you're going to the office, even though your commute may not be more than ten steps from the bedroom to the home office. Indeed, there are a number of people who, although they may not dress up as much as they would if they were going in to the company office for the day, will still dress for working at home. They may just forget about the mascara or wear sneakers with a suit, but they will still dress, to a degree, for work.

Which Day(s) of the Week?

When you first start to telecommute, it's best to take things slowly. Pick a day where you know most of your work can be done at home. Ease into your day by doing some reading to help you make the transition from your personal at-home self to your working-at-home self.

The next day, head for the office. Meet with your supervisor to discuss how your telecommuting day went, both the pros and the cons. If you want to continue to telecommute, state that you'd like to try it again next week. As the weeks go on, you'll feel more comfortable working from home, and you'll get used to making the transition to your work self in the morning and back to your personal self at night.

You may want to keep your telecommuting schedule informal and work at home on an as-needed basis. Many people, however, appreciate having a regular weekly schedule and knowing where they'll be on a particular day. Your customers and coworkers will appreciate it, too. The only question is, which days?

Many telecommuters like to alternate an at-home day with a day in the office. Some people don't like to miss more than one day in a row in the office, fearing coworkers will adopt an out-of-sight, out-of-mind mentality. Someone who works at home two days a week would spend Monday,

Wednesday, and Friday in the office and Tuesday and Thursday at home. Others prefer to stay home two or more days in a row because of the type of work they do there and view a day in between spent in the office as an interruption of the project they're working on.

Taking a Break

Whenever you work in a main office, even though you may not take an official "coffee break," chances are that your entire workday is punctuated by regular interruptions—visits with coworkers, phone calls, errands, meetings—that help break up your routine and keep you from working too long on one thing. Breaks are both good and bad—they help to keep your mind fresh, but they can also prevent you from getting much work done. The lack of interruptions at home accounts for much of the increased productivity many telecommuters report. However, you do need occasional breaks in your day to relax and recharge.

One way to take a break is to vary the kinds of work you plan to do each day. Write for an hour or two, then make a few phone calls, then read over a couple of pertinent new journal articles that just came out that week. It's also important to get away from your work altogether now and then by going to the kitchen for a cup of tea or going for a walk. Even fifteen minutes will do it. If you don't need to be by the phones constantly, you may even want to take a long lunch hour, eat at the local coffee shop, then pick up a few groceries or the dry cleaning on the way back.

If your schedule is flexible, you can take your lunch earlier or later than usual in order to avoid the crowds. However, many telecommuters say that even a quick walk around the block is enough for them to clear their heads or give them some perspective on a particular problem that had been bothering them all morning.

Some people also take a break by exercising. It's easier to exercise regularly when you're working from home than when you're in the office because you probably won't have to fight locker-room gridlock or the post-aerobic traffic jam in the shower.

No matter what your reasons are for taking a break, the important thing is that you indeed do it. If you don't, the dearth of built-in interruptions in a telecommuter's lifestyle means that you may burn out and find yourself back in the office full-time, which you probably don't want.

Balancing Your Home and Work Lives

When it comes to the topic of working in the same place that you live, you'll probably get one of two reactions: "That sounds great" or "Ugh, that would be awful." Rarely do you find a person who is neutral about the topic of working at home or anywhere except a traditional office setting. Sometimes, however, a negative reaction stems from the fact that a person's studio apartment is crammed to the hilt already, which would leave no room for a home office.

For other people, however, the problem lies in the belief that home is for the personal side of life. They have no desire to let the 9-to-5 grind permeate their domestic walls. Some people will not be convinced that it's actually possible to combine work and home under one roof—*theirs*. For those who are interested in the concept but need a little guidance in how to mesh the two successfully, here's some help.

In order to get used to doing work in a space that you once solely associated with time away from the office, the first thing you need to do is draw a distinct line between your home office and your living space (see Chapter 5). If this isn't possible—for instance, if your at-home work space is relegated to the dining room table—then you should try to gather your work into a box or closet at the end of each workday and especially on the weekends. Set small goals for yourself and reward yourself when you've completed them. For instance, promise yourself that when you finish working on a report, you'll take a walk around the block. Such benefits are necessary in order to balance your home and work lives so that your living space doesn't just turn into a work space.

To help their employees keep their personal lives in perspective, some companies actually won't allow anyone to telecommute five days a week. It's best if you come into the office once or twice a week so you can keep up ongoing interactions with your coworkers. It's important to keep these interactions going.

Ann Bacon, a sales rep for Farmland Foods in Kansas City, told *Forbes* magazine about the downside of working from home: "You can't leave it behind because it's always there." Her husband usually decides when it's time for her to break camp, coming into her home office and telling her it's time for dinner. You may need a similar type of "alarm clock" in order to keep you from working too much overtime.

Gina Dickinson of Aetna says she is happy telecommuting but adds that it's not always easy. "Telecommuting sounds wonderful to everybody, but it does require a lot of planning and balance on my part," she says. "And it also places extra demands on my family as well. For instance, if I don't get enough work done one day, my husband has to take over with the baby that night while I go back on the computer. But that's the price I have to pay for it, and I don't have to commute. I don't have the expense of day care, and I can be at home, which is important to me."

PROFILE OF A TELECOMMUTER: MICHAEL GORODEZKY

Michael Gorodezky is the president of PSP Information Systems, a software and systems vendor that specializes in patient tracking, billing, and case management. The company is located in Oakland, California, but Gorodezky runs it from his home office in Nashville. Here's the way it happened:

"In 1990, my wife took a job in Nashville as director of a local hospice," he says. "At that time I planned to take another job when we moved, but we decided that I could stay with the company and telecommute. I was a senior vice president at the company specializing in project management and support for customers on product development. In 1993 the president of the company became ill and they asked me to return to California to take over the company." He did for awhile, but in late 1994 he was preparing to move back to Nashville and go to California periodically and still run the company as president, even though he doesn't feel that he can adequately do that job from this far away. He plans to stay on temporarily as president and to appoint a COO to provide for continuity.

In addition to running the company, Gorodezky works on new business development, investigating partnerships between PSP and other companies. He says he can do this part of his job as easily from Nashville as from Oakland. He also gets involved in sales and marketing as a support person, and when another employee identifies a new customer, he will help out on presentations or do them himself.

This is his first telecommuting experience. "By the end of three years, I had gone through an evolution," he says. "I had reached a level of comfort that wasn't there in the beginning. At first I was paranoid about the whole thing because I was worried about what people thought; maybe they thought I had a cushy deal or something, which is probably one of the things that telecommuters always worry about. I also worried about my position in the company, which was pretty stupid because they named me president." He looks back and sees that many people at the company didn't improve their positions despite working in the main office. Gorodezky didn't hurt his position by telecommuting; in fact, the contributions he made got him promoted. "It was clear to everybody after I was made president that even after I stopped being president, I would go back to telecommuting because of the revenue I brought in," he says. "And that was just fine with me."

To keep in touch with the office, Gorodezky calls in several times each day. In fact, he says he often knows more about what is going on in the company than people who work in the main office because employees tend to use him as a hub for a lot of things. "You'd think people there would know everything, though," he adds.

The biggest advantage telecommuting provided him with was the ability to earn a California salary in a part of the country that couldn't pay one. He adds that it was to the company's advantage to keep him, with his ten years of experience in the field. "And whatever the disadvantage was, it was offset by the fact that they had a skilled person there doing the work which they couldn't have replaced very easily," he says. "I have a Ph.D. in psychology and have worked in computers for twenty years, and there aren't a lot of people out there like me. There would have been a high cost associated with replacing me. The continuity was good for both of us."

Gorodezky says the employees at the company have easily accepted his telecommuting arrangement. Almost everyone in the company has a second phone line and a PC terminal at home, though no one there telecommutes on a regular basis. "Once we had a situation with heavy rains where somebody called in and worked from home for a couple of days, but we don't have anybody who telecommutes

Monday through Friday," he says. "More often, it's because of overtime or the need to check on something. Occasionally, it's because someone's kid is sick. We offered the opportunity to some people, but they didn't want it. I was surprised, because it seems like commuting is a big pain, but some people like getting out of the house."

Initially, Gorodezky let work interfere with some of his personal life. "For a long time, due to time zone differences, I let people interrupt my dinner and early evening with their phone calls. If they were on the West Coast, they'd put off calling me until the end of their day," he says. "At first, I'd jump whenever the phone rang, and there were times when I actually felt guilty for not answering it. Now, I let voice mail pick up if I'm having dinner or relaxing." He adds that it took him awhile to figure that out. One way he solved this problem was to train his coworkers back in California to call him earlier in the day rather than later so that he wouldn't be working fourteen-hour days. "I work more when I'm telecommuting than when I work at the office, because basically there's nothing else to do," he says.

Gorodezky says he wakes up and starts working immediately. "It wasn't unusual for me to take just ten or fifteen minutes off for lunch, then work for the rest of the day," he says. "And I don't think I turned the TV on during the day once in three years when I was working at home. I just decided it was not a good idea, not the type of habit a telecommuter would want to cultivate." He also tried to keep all of his work in his home office rather than letting it migrate into the rest of the house.

"If you like going to work and being with your friends, then you're going to have a hard time with telecommuting," says Gorodezky. "The phone can replace some of it, but it isn't the same as being there. I think that it's completely appropriate for you to go for a walk in the middle of the day and get some exercise to clear your head, and don't consider yourself to be goofing off. After all, you do work more, and you don't have the commute or the transitional time coming and going.

"Doing something that's good for yourself is also doing something that's good for your work," he continues. "It is so different from what you'd do in an office setting that it seems very self-indulgent, but it really isn't. I would frequently go for two to three hours with nothing to distract me, and there's nothing like that in the office. There, the distractions are almost continuous, so you have to learn how to work in between them."

Telecommuting Snapshot

Back in the mid-1980s, a planned development in California called Eaglecrest was touted with much fanfare as a telecommuting community of the future. The developers envisioned 360 private homes in all, each one specifically wired with special cables and extra phone lines to enable the residents to work from home. Later developments included a PBX system that would essentially provide each home with the phone capabilities of a standard office, from call forwarding to intercom services and multiple phones using one line. Future plans also included a videoconferencing system via satellite. The developer primarily targeted buyers working for technology companies in the Silicon Valley and Sacramento, as well as consultants, who ordinarily prefer to work at home. Unfortunately, this telecommuting dream was cut short when the developer declared bankruptcy after building only two of the houses. Another developer subsequently stepped in to finish a scaled-back version of this ambitious project.

7

Working with the Office

At Chiat/Day, a worldwide advertising agency with offices in New York and Los Angeles, owner Jay Chiat—who works most of the time from Venice, California—prefers his employees to telecommute. When they do come in to the office, they encounter something resembling a library in format. An employee checks out a locker, a computer, and a phone for the day. At the end of the day, all are returned.

In an interview that appeared in the July 1994 issue of *Wired* magazine, Chiat revealed his egalitarian strategies. "You come to work because the office is a resource," he told writer David Dix. "The office is a place where you can meet with other people, and the office has libraries of books and information on CD-ROM that might help you with your work." He encourages everyone at the agency to view the office the same way. "No one really gets any special treatment," he says. "No one gets a corner office to put pictures of their family and their dog in. Everyone answers their own phones and makes their own coffee."

He likens the organization of his business to a university because people can pretty much come and go as they please. Chiat believes the majority of U.S. companies treat their employees like elementary school students. "You go to work and you only leave your office when you have to go to the bathroom," he told *Wired*. "That sort of thing breeds insularity and fear, and it's nonproductive. The important thing to focus on is what kind of work you do."

In addition, Chiat urges his employees to bring their information and research out into the open, to produce it in database and CD-ROM format for other employees to share instead of using it once and then sticking it in a desk drawer. His approach encourages teamwork, and the information can be put onto laptops and brought home so that telecommuting employees can have a wealth of resources within easy reach.

Working With Customers

One issue that frequently arises around the office when the subject turns to telecommuters—especially full-time telecommuters—is that attention to the customer will become diffused if employees are not gathered together and toiling toward a common goal. Inattention could result in mixed results on team-oriented projects, crossed signals, and unnecessary turmoil both at the office and at the home offices of telecommuters.

Not to worry. When IBM dispersed the majority of its sales staff to home and mobile offices and set up a warehouse-like facility as a telework center, one concern of managers and employees was that each customer's needs wouldn't be communicated to fellow workers in order to come up with the best solution. Management came up with the idea of conducting regular weekly lunch meetings as well as a daylong workshop and seminar that's held once every three months, to reestablish face-to-face contact and share success stories as well as failures.

When You Do Visit the Office

Make it easy for your coworkers to forget that you're working at home. Use the time that you spend in the office not only to do whatever work you need to do, but also to attend meetings and participate in gossip. Yes, it takes effort to keep your name and ideas in front of others at the office—unless you're the boss—but it's worth it. Take a coworker to lunch or go out with your colleagues on the days you spend in the office. Drop by others' desks and offices to gossip, and try to encourage coworkers to schedule meetings on the days when you're going to be in. Of course, you don't want to go to the other extreme and make your colleagues wish you were telecommuting Monday through Friday; be just intrusive enough so that you're not out of sight, out of mind.

Towards the end of the 1990s, as telecommuting and other flexible workstyles become more common and ingrained in American corporate culture, you won't have to work as hard at maintaining contact with coworkers. But if you're among the telecommuting pioneers at your company, you should expect to spend extra hours being social whenever you're in the office.

AT&T's Business Network Sales Division closed down, consolidated, or reduced office space in ten states in 1991. Today, telecommuting employees who need to touch down in the office occasionally find a workplace that looks drastically different from what they remember. Temporary cubicles dot the floor, and only a handful of standard desks are sprinkled throughout the office, all designated for managers. There's also a conference room for private meetings, but my favorite part of AT&T's redesign is the little patch of Velcro on the wall of each cubicle, intended for an employee to attach his or her nameplate to during an office visit.

Software for Your Boss

If you're interested in telecommuting for your current company, chances are that some coworkers are, too. If they're not specifically interested in telecommuting, they may be interested in exploring another type of flexible employment arrangement, such as job sharing, a compressed work week, or even part-time employment. However, your company may object to the extra work and hassle involved in tracking every employee who's not working the traditional forty-hour week. After all, telecommuting and other flexible work arrangements do force you and your manager to do extra work to document your progress on certain projects.

One way to help you and your boss keep track of your work and contact is by keeping a log, written in a notebook or in a computer file. Each day that you work at home should be documented as should each time you talk to your manager. Each entry should include a few words describing the particular day you telecommuted, the work you did, when you spoke to your manager, and what you discussed.

Though it is possible to keep track in this fashion, there's a computer program for Windows that makes everything a bit easier. The program, called Flex-It, helps companies keep track of all employees who are telecommuting and participating in other flexible work situations, provides a network for the employees and their managers, and helps companies create customized training of employees and supervisors. Flex-It offers a toll-free service that both employees and managers can call to ask questions and receive new research into the field. The program requires Microsoft

Windows 3.1 or higher, a 386SX PC or higher, at least 4 MB of RAM, DOS 3.3 or higher, a minimum of 10 MB hard disk space, an EGA display monitor, and a mouse. For more information, call Sandra Sullivan at Flex-It, (203) 243-1142, or write to Flex-It, 159 Autumn Drive, Southington, CT 06489.

Donna Cunningham at Bell Labs has communication down to a science. Anybody, anywhere, can reach her whether they call her home office number or the General Bell Labs number down in New Jersey.

"Calls are forwarded to my home line if I'm using my business line, and my home line has Call Waiting for when both lines are in use," she says. It's important that Cunningham, a media relations manager who wants to be responsive to the press seven days a week and most hours of the day as well, not miss any calls. She also has a fax machine and can be reached via e-mail, and she uses a videophone, supplied by AT&T, for her weekly department meeting. Easy access is the key to her job, she says, even though the home office is 400 miles from her doorstep.

Give This to Your Boss

Although you and your boss may have approached your telecommuting arrangement with open minds, you may run into problems down the road that involve management styles as well as productivity. The following suggestions will help your manager keep that open mind that is so necessary to a successful telecommuting arrangement.

☐ Make sure that you meet regularly with your employee whenever he or she is in the office. Face-to-face contact is invaluable in maintaining a good working relationship.

❑ Develop a checklist that will tell both employee and manager what to look for in terms of the work to be produced at home and that to be done in the office. Make your priorities clear but feel free to change them if, for instance, the employee finds it difficult to work at home because it's too quiet.

❑ Regularly check back with your proposal to match your intentions with your goals. Are you straying too much from the amount and type of work you outlined specifically for your proposal?

❑ Review why you decided to let your employee tele-commute in the first place. Have your reasons remained the same, or have other advantages over-shadowed the benefits you originally projected?

❑ Are you changing your ideas about employees who telecommute as you work with them, or are you unintentionally—or intentionally—sabotaging your employees with your preconceived notions? Unless you give your telecommuters some slack and trust them to do what they've said they're going to do, it's not going to work out for the long run.

❑ Make sure you weigh a task very carefully before you say that a telecommuter won't be able to handle it because of proximity. Take care not to discriminate subconsciously against a telecommuting employee because he or she is not in the office Monday through Friday.

❑ Learn to give feedback to telecommuters. Even though telecommuters may be able to work well by themselves, that doesn't negate their need for feed-back. In fact, they may need even more of it in the beginning as they work out a rhythm with you. The best way to give feedback is on the phone and by e-mail or fax. Some managers prefer to save positive feedback for e-mail and fax and deliver negative feedback, which requires more detail and give-and-take, on the phone or perhaps in person the next time the employee is in the office.

A manager or supervisor who telecommutes him- or herself begins to analyze the work of his or her own employees with a more results-oriented eye, whether they telecommute or not. Put in simple terms, managers who telecommute not only judge their own work with an eye for results, but also judge their employees' accomplishments.

Working with telecommuters requires the boss to incorporate a little bit of flexibility into his or her workstyle. For instance, Susan Herman of the City of Los Angeles says an agreement is developed between supervisor and employee specifying that a certain degree of training will take place. "We train employees, bosses, and then train them together," she says. "And training is critical because it means that people can ferret out their issues in advance and begin to think about which jobs are conducive to telecommuting. For instance, someone might tell an employee that he can't telecommute on Tuesdays because the department always holds its staff meetings on Tuesdays. Well, my thought is, 'Why is it on Tuesdays? What's special about Tuesdays? Why couldn't you do it on Wednesdays?' We also have found that when employees and managers perform a task breakdown of their jobs, some people get in touch with their jobs for the first time ever. As a result, some supervisors find out for the first time what their employees are really doing."

Emily Bassman says focusing on objectives and results is the key for managers and supervisors, and not only when telecommuting is involved. "Setting clear objectives and understanding the telecommuting arrangement is the first priority," she says. "The manager should do whatever is necessary to feel comfortable that the telecommuter is doing his or her work. No one admits to managing by whether or not they can see your face in the office, but this is still part of the American culture. Because of telecommuting, managers have to begin to think in a different way. It doesn't really matter if you can see an employee at his desk or not. There's no guarantee that they're being productive. What you have to look at is what that person produces."

PROFILE OF A TELECOMMUTING RELATIONSHIP: FRANK DAMICO AND RICH WACHUNIS

Rich Wachunis is a programmer with the information systems department at Bell Atlantic, based in Freehold, New Jersey. He's been with the company since 1974. Frank Damico, his supervisor, works at corporate headquarters in Maryland. In 1992 Rich was offered a particular assignment that gave him the opportunity to telecommute five days a week from his home. He took it.

"I believe that Rich approached me on the issue of telecommuting," says Damico. "I was open to the idea, but I had to make sure that certain criteria were met. I wanted to feel certain that the job and responsibilities that Rich had lent themselves to telecommuting, but this wasn't a problem since I was familiar with his duties. I also talked with him to make sure he was focused. But more importantly, I had to make sure that his environment at home would lend itself to telecommuting. Rich did his homework in that area, as he researched corporate policy and addressed all the issues. It turned out to be a real nondecision, because he was a very good fit for telecommuting."

"The type of work I was doing at the time didn't require face-to-face contact with other people," says Rich. "And I had a home environment that was very well suited to working at home." He started out telecommuting two days a week, but it worked so well that he soon expanded to four or five days a week.

"The company supplied me with phone lines. One of the company's policies is that the equipment you use at your home is your responsibility. If special software is needed to access files at work, they supply that. But the PC is my responsibility," he said. "I already had a computer, and I upgraded it so that I could take advantage of newer technology. I also bought a couple of two-line phones, one to put in the office and another in the kitchen. I felt it was important to be as accessible as possible at home, more so than in the office." In all, Wachunis says, he spent about $3,000 on equipment, though he admits that it's not necessary to spend that much.

Frank says that when it came to managing Rich as a telecommuter, the only difference was in the techniques he used to communicate with him. "Obviously, with someone who's sitting close to you in the office, you can shout over the cubicle or walk over to see them," he said. "And your conversations tend to be impromptu, but they can also be disruptive. With a telecommuter, I usually have to sit down and take a few minutes and think about what I have to say. I thought the communicating that Rich and I did was better than a lot of the communicating I do in the office.

"Rich would be in touch with me via e-mail or voice mail maybe twice a day, and I tried to contact him several times a week. If there were general announcements, I would forward them to Rich. I didn't visit his home office, though we talked about it. He made himself very accessible during business hours, and I felt that he was far more productive at home than in the office. In fact, the biggest difference was that it was easier to contact him at home; he tended to be away from his desk more in the office. At home he was right there by the telephone. The fact that he was cut off from normal company mail and support systems was a big issue for him."

"Before I started to telecommute, the company had started to give telecommuting seminars to help people to make the adjustment," says Rich. "One thing they said there was that you cannot effectively work for corporate America at home in your pajamas and that you have to make a mental transition in order to work. So I did get dressed every day. What I dressed in was not what I would go to the office in, but it was part of a routine I did to get myself mentally prepared for work."

He did keep the same hours at home as in the main office. "I found that I wasn't taking as long a lunch, maybe fifteen minutes, since the food was right there in the kitchen. And if the phone rang while I was eating, I would answer it," he said.

"I still tried to go in one day a week or every other week because I missed the social life," he says. At times he would call people on the phone to socialize. Rich discussed this point before he started telecommuting, so the other people in his group knew that he would sometimes call just to chat. Nonetheless, he felt he had fallen out of the social loop. He would communicate with Frank through voice and e-mail, and although Rich understood what Frank was saying, he feels that he did not get the group's impression of what Frank had said, and that was an important thing to maintain.

He says that the biggest disadvantage to telecommuting is missing out on the gossip mill. There's probably as much information that circulates through the rumor mill as anywhere else, and he says he lost a certain amount of that because he wasn't directly in the office. "It wasn't really a big deal because the corporation was going through some major changes, and any time there's a change, people have angst about it and the rumors fly," he says. "By not being exposed to it, I probably had less stress and was more productive than people in the office who heard it all.

"Other people in our district started to telecommute after I did, but they usually kept it to only one or two days a week," he says. "The biggest thing I told them is that you have to maintain communication. It's your responsibility to make sure your manager knows what you are doing, how you're getting it done, when you're getting it done, and how successful you are with it. I would also let him know about a particular accomplishment or if I had run into a problem somewhere. In essence, I had to play the game a little bit more than I would have otherwise because telecommuting is still new to a lot of people. If I worked extra hours, I made sure he got a message from me from that out-of-hours time frame."

He was concerned that because he was telecommuting, he would be the forgotten man in the office. "That was always on my mind, and maybe I overcompensated, but it worked quite well," he says.

"There's also the cultural feeling out there that if you're telecommuting, you're getting away with something," he adds. "In fact, this was sometimes said in jest by some members of my group, but they did feel that there was some truth to it: 'Rich is at home and therefore he's got it easier.' And I think that also is true the further you go up the corporate ladder. But if people have worked with a telecommuter, their attitudes change. If it's just something they've read about, I don't think they've had a grand awakening yet."

Frank telecommutes at his job as well, spending a day at home every week or two. "I try and save tasks that I think need a little more thought, or writing, or appraisals or letters for home," he says. "I have fewer disruptions at home than at the office. I don't necessarily contact my supervisor from home, unless I need to. I do contact my employees via voice mail a couple of times during the day. On occasion it's far more productive for me to work from home than to commute to the office."

Rich admits that telecommuting may have had a slight effect on his compensation for the year he was telecommuting. "Possibly, if I'd been in the office doing what I did, it may have been perceived as a bigger accomplishment," he says. "Not by Frank, but by other managers in the district. I think that some of the other managers who aren't familiar with telecommuting may perceive that I must not be working as hard if I'm not in the office every day. And looking back at it, I did have some minor responsibilities that involved some contact with the other managers. I think that finding more opportunities to have contact with those people might have helped them to realize the value I was providing."

The thing he liked most about telecommuting was the informality and the lack of structure. "It's more comfortable," he says. "I can wear what I want, and I'm not distracted by other things in the office. If I feel like playing the radio while I'm working, I can. And if I think of something after hours that's a real quick fix, I have everything at my fingertips to try something right then and there. Having the resources available and not having to go back in to the office at night or stay at the office late if I needed to work overtime is a real advantage. I can break for dinner for an hour or two and go back and work another couple of hours. If I was in the office, I would have had to stay and trudge through that extra hour or two after a full day's work."

He says that one problem he encountered was that his mail still went to his office. "If I only went to the office once a week and something important came in while I was gone, that was a problem," he says. "It was also an inconvenience to some of my coworkers to have to share printed material with me for that reason. They could fax it to me, but it wasn't as easy as just dropping it off at my desk. There were several people in my town—Toms River—who also worked in Freehold, where my office was. One of them was also a telecommuter, so he understood the priority for me. If he was in the office and I knew that some important mail had come in, then he would pick it up at my office and bring it back to Toms River for me.

"A lot of people at work perceived that I had big savings because I wasn't driving my car to work, but my utility bills went up. I also found out it was worth insuring my computer at home for business use; since I was using it for business, it isn't necessarily covered under homeowner's insurance."

Another problem he found when he first started telecommuting was that his wife was home. "There had to be a functional separation between my being home when I'm working and my being home when I'm off," he said. "It was very easy for her to walk into my office and interrupt me. We had to set down ground rules: When I'm working, I'm working. For awhile, I even asked her to call me on the phone if she needed to talk to me.

"The biggest surprise I had was how many things I always left behind in the office," he says. "I ended up duplicating a lot of reference material so I could have it at home. I think it's easier to work the majority of the time at home. I think it would be more difficult to work two days here, three days in the office, etc. Then I would forever have to think about what I needed in order to work somewhere else."

"I think that telecommuting is a great opportunity because it puts more responsibility on the employee, who then has to manage his life better," says Rich. "I have learned to remove myself from the chores at home when I go to work in my home office. One of the things I discovered early on was to take all of my personal work, like my checking account and my insurance papers, and get them out of the office before I started to work. I wouldn't have them in my office in Freehold, so it was inappropriate to have them in my home office."

Even though he loves it, Wachunis doesn't think that telecommuting is for everybody. "There are people and situations for whom it won't work," he says. "But there's more opportunity for it than people realize; they're just not open-minded enough to see how well it will work. For instance, there are some people who can't get beyond getting up from their desks and walking over to another desk with a person at it and looking them in the eye and saying, 'I need this or that.' Instead, I pick up the phone or send a fax or e-mail, and we can share the same information almost as fast. After all, the technology is there."

"During the winter of 1994, with all the snow, a lot of people tried to get to work, couldn't manage it, and the company lost a lot of productivity. I got to work, worked a full day and was fully functional. I think as more people do it, it will become more accepted," says Rich.

Staying Connected

Deciding to work from home, even full-time, doesn't mean that you have to totally cut yourself off from the office. The flex-time and job-sharing programs instituted by many companies in the 1980s provided a way for employees—particularly parents—to scale back at work while still keeping a hand in what's going on at the office. Telecommuting operates on the same premise. If these programs exist at your company, pointing to them as a way to increase productivity and keep employees happy may be just the thing that puts your boss over the edge and makes him or her grant your request to telecommute.

Agreeing to touch base with the office frequently will help keep you in sight and in mind of your colleagues and soothe your boss's fears that your workload may diminish. In fact, with technology developing the way it is today, you can work at home or elsewhere and still keep in touch even if you can't get to the office.

Elizabeth Suneby chose to stay in close contact with her company, Work/Family Directions in Boston, during her maternity leave by telecommuting part-time. When she joined the company in November 1992 as vice president in charge of marketing, she was four months pregnant, which the company was aware of when she was hired. She left in the beginning of April 1993 for fourteen weeks of maternity leave, a little over half of which was paid.

Though the company didn't require it of her, Suneby wanted to keep in touch with her colleagues during her break, and she even interviewed several job candidates at her home at one point. "As the head of a department, and also since I was relatively new, I wanted to be on top of certain things," she said. Suneby had a fax machine at home, and chose to work on certain projects, keeping the option of passing on projects if she felt too overwhelmed.

Before she went on leave, she identified the major projects that were underway or were scheduled to begin while she was gone, and she specified the staff member who would head up each project, with another employee who would act as support. "Everyone warned me against committing myself to all that I thought I could do, and because this was my first baby, I didn't know what to expect," she said. "My coworkers left phone mail and faxes for me, and I had the option of picking them up or not."

Work/Family Directions is a very employee-friendly company; it made *Working Mother* magazine's annual Top 100 Companies to Work For list several times. Her superiors gave Suneby the option of bailing out if and when she wanted to, and she definitely appreciated the flexibility. For the first three months of her leave she wanted to stay connected to what was going on in the office. But when the end of her leave was nearing, she decided to disconnect totally and announced a self-imposed two-week blackout period.

"The core belief at the company is that you have to help people balance work and family to get the most out of your employees," she says. "I work very intensely and am just as serious about my career since becoming a mother, but I have a much better perspective and will probably do even a better job because I have more diversity in my life." Before she temporarily left the main office, Suneby worked hard to get her department in order, in terms of both handling the workload and assigning certain responsibilities that needed to be covered in her absence. "Do what you can beforehand to feel good about leaving things at work," she says. "It's important for the company, for yourself, and, if you're a manager, for the people who work for you."

Being Flexible

When I write a book, I draw up a proposal and table of contents, but I know that by the time I've written the last word, the content of the book will barely resemble that early outline. I will have tried out new ideas during the writing process, experimented. It's important to be similarly flexible when telecommuting, to vary your routine and discover the ways in which you work best. Think of those studies conducted to determine whether a person is a "lark" who works better during the day or an "owl" who functions better at night. I've never known how owls are able to get anything done during lark time, and vice versa.

When you first become comfortable with telecommuting, it's a good idea to experiment with a variety of work styles. Work in spurts, spending perhaps only an hour on one part of your project before you switch to something else; then do all of your work in one sitting until you're done. If you favor one type of work habit, try the opposite to see how you do. Being flexible about how you work will help keep your job interesting.

Half-Time Analysis

After you've been telecommuting for a couple of months and you've had some time to reflect, it's a good idea to evaluate your experience and identify the areas where you've met or exceeded your goals and other areas where you would like to do better.

The purpose of evaluating your telecommuting arrangement? To see what is working and what isn't and adjust your work style accordingly, and to decide whether you want to continue telecommuting for your current employer. A close analysis at this stage will help you improve in the areas you feel you fall short in and to appreciate the parts that you enjoy most and do best.

Performing this half-time analysis will also help you decide how you're going to change your telecommuting arrangement from that point on, if at all. Be honest and answer the following questions in your notebook in as much detail as you want.

1. Do you feel you've accomplished the main goals you set out to reach? How so?

2. List the five most important things you've learned about your work and yourself so far as a result of telecommuting, and tell how you learned them.

3. List five things you didn't accomplish but wanted to. How would you rearrange your telecommuting arrangement to place more priority on them?

4. What do you want to do differently from now on, if anything? What do you want to remain the same?

5. What are you going to do now with what you've learned?

Holding on to What You've Gained

Your work pattern at home differs from the routine you follow when you go into the office. Though you may vow to assimilate some of your at-home habits when you work at corporate headquarters, it's very hard not to slip back into your old, sometimes destructive habits once you step off the elevator. How can you prevent this from happening?

First, look at your half-time telecommuting analysis, specifically the list of things you've learned. If it helps to make a sign and hang it up at work or put some reminders where they're never more than an arm's length away, do it. This will help you to be aware of when you're slipping into your pre-telecommuting habits back at the office. Work to cut down on interruptions by closing the door, having voice mail pick up your calls, and being just a little less social. However, don't go off in the other direction and feel and act superior because you're telecommuting and everyone else in the office isn't. Don't get preachy about telecommuting. As the cliché goes, people will get it if you live by example.

Take a breather each day that you spend working in the office and try to assume the attitude you have when you're working from home. This daily reinforcement may be the best way to keep things in perspective.

Security

Security is often a sticky topic when it comes to employees who work from home. Inevitably, they're going to work on some topics that are confidential. If their kids use the home computer to play computer games and accidentally stumble upon a secret document, it's a breach of confidentiality even if they have no idea what they're looking at. And if you're hooked into the office LAN system or use one of the commercial online services, there's always the (admittedly remote) chance that someone may try to break into your computer and open confidential documents.

You'll need to determine in advance with your boss how you're going to handle confidential materials when working from home. Of course, the easiest thing to do is simply to not bring these high-security documents home, but sometimes that cannot be avoided. You can store the documents on floppy disks and transfer them to the office yourself, but don't forget to make backup files. Will you send them to the office to be backed up, will you use a tape drive, or will you simply save them as backup documents on your computer's hard drive?

It may not be necessary, but you'll have to consider whether you'll need a paper shredder at home, especially if you work at a high level in your company and if competition in your industry is so acute that you wouldn't put it past your rivals to go snooping in your garbage cans at home.

If you signed a confidentiality statement when you were first hired or when you began work on a particular high-security project, you may need to review it with your supervisor and company attorney to check if it also applies to the work you do at home or if it's necessary to draw up an entirely new statement.

Measuring the Results

Telecommuters are evaluated more by what they produce than by how or where they produce it. Their work can be measured in a number of different ways. If, for instance, a telecommuter spends a majority of the time on the phone making sales calls, a manager might evaluate his or her progress by looking at the dollar amount of the employee's phone bills and the number of sales that come in as a result of his or her calls.

Most often, the criteria used to judge the work of telecommuters concern the completion of certain projects. Supervisors monitor how far along the employee is in completing the various stages of a given project. Regular communication can help the employee, supervisor, and coworker to determine how on track the telecommuter is and to help troubleshoot when it's clear the project is not going to be completed within the original specified time frame. Some managers like to set goals and objectives at the beginning of a business cycle (every quarter, for example), whereas others go strictly by the deadlines involved in each individual project.

Dealing With Ornery People Back at the Office

One unfortunate problem you may run into is that many managers base their evaluations on the old-fashioned basis—immediate physical proximity. They think that because you're not working in the office five days a week, eight hours a day, your job must not be as important as those of employees who work in the office. A manager who falls into this category may decide that you don't have to be involved when the time comes to make important decisions.

You may find that important decisions have been made that concern you and your responsibilities at the company and that you had no say in them simply because you were not there.

In this case, you should continue to stay in touch as much as you can with your coworkers in the department, asking about new developments and other important day-to-day changes. Offer your two cents, both to your colleagues and to the indifferent manager. Then, when an important decision is just around the bend and everybody gets together to discuss it, one of your coworkers may point out that you're not there and urge the supervisor to bring you in on the phone. Of course, the manager may be so difficult that your colleagues don't want to point out the error of his ways, but they will still get back to you after the meeting and report to you in full on the contents. Then you can e-mail the manager with your comments and questions. He may be surprised that you know what was discussed, and a situation such as this can develop into a nasty power struggle. But if it's important to you to be included in important decisions, then you have to do what is necessary.

However, managers across the board have reported that working with telecommuters improves their managerial skills overall. Managing an employee from afar basically forces them to become clearer about their goals, communicate in a more effective way, and focus on attaining results rather than taking attendance. An added incentive to managers whose employees are considering telecommuting is that much of the burden of supervision falls to the telecommuter, which relieves the supervisor of some of the work. It's now up to the employee to meet quotas, maintain contact with colleagues back at the office, and stay accessible.

Tips for a Smooth Transition

It will be awkward at first while people get used to working with you from afar, over phones, modems, and faxes. Here are some things you can tell your supervisor and coworkers to make things run a little bit more smoothly.

The first thing you should do is to consider your telecommuting to be taking place within a probationary period. Who knows? No matter how much you may think you will enjoy working out of your home, you may end up hating it and wishing that you had never thought of it. Even if you have the right kind of personality for telecommuting (see chapter 3), you may have overlooked some things in your eagerness to avoid a two-hour one-way commute or to spend more time with your family.

So look at your telecommuting as an initial trial period of two months or so. At the end of that time, you'll be well positioned to examine the pros and cons of working from home and discuss them with your manager and coworkers. I'd suggest that you not make changes before then, however, even if some parts of the experience are not comfortable for you. You'll need some time to adjust to the rhythms of your week, to fall into a day-to-day work pattern and a routine of maintaining contact with the office. At the end of two months, both you and your officemates will be able to offer critical feedback that may not be applicable if the trial telecommuting period is for a shorter period of time.

Plan to chart your progress on a daily, weekly, and/or monthly basis. Decide in advance with your colleagues how much work you can realistically expect to accomplish within these time frames, and be sure to keep in touch with the office about whether you are meeting your goals, exceeding them, or having trouble keeping up. Then be realistic about whether your working from home was the primary culprit in keeping you from succeeding or whether the workload of the particular project was just too heavy. Be prepared to adjust accordingly.

By charting your progress, you will be helping to train your manager to judge your performance by results, not by your physical presence in the office, which is how the majority of managers rate their employees. In this respect, the men and women who supervise telecommuters ease their own workload; instead of hovering over their employees, hounding them over every detail, the manager becomes a mentor to his employee. The stress turns from how the work gets done to getting it done well, which comes as a relief for most employees and managers.

A sneaky way to teleconference with an employee back at the office is to log on to one of the commercial online services and then take advantage of its forum and bulletin board services to hold ongoing conversations. Such give-and-take is impossible with e-mail; one person types in a question or answer and sends it, and the other person has to get the signal that mail has arrived and open that message before responding. The online services make it possible for people to conduct an ongoing dialogue. For example, with America Online all you have to do is to enter one of the "lobbies" under the People Connection headline, make sure your colleague is in the same lobby, and then enter a private room within that lobby to hold your discussion.

It's important for telecommuters to make regular contact with coworkers and bosses in person because telecommuting, despite its effectiveness and increased productivity, still allows for only one-dimensional communication. Experts say that when two people have a conversation, only about 20 percent of the communication is through the spoken word. The rest comes from nonverbal and body language, which is nonexistent in most telecommuting situations and greatly diminished even if you use videoconferencing on a regular basis. For this reason, many career counselors suggest that most telecommuters limit the number of days they work at home to two or three. You actually miss a great deal of the essence of what is being discussed if your only avenues of communication are the phone, fax, and e-mail.

Telecommuters should ask themselves the following questions:

How will you get information from your home office to the main office? Will you use fax, phone, modem, e-mail, or regular mail, or will you bring it in on the days that you visit the office? What will you do in emergencies? Are there some projects for which one form of transmission is preferable over another, or is it more a matter of the time frame in which the project needs to be completed? Who will you select to serve as your backup in the office when customers call or when a particular package or paper needs to be sent from the office?

Ask your coworkers about the concerns they have if you start to work from home either full- or part-time. Are they jealous of you? Do they think that they're going to be saddled with more work if you're out of the office more? Do they feel they'll be more likely to be promoted if you're out of their way? (They'll never answer in the affirmative to this last question, so don't ask it. Instead, you should watch for clues in their mannerisms that they do indeed feel this way.) Get a realistic idea of their concerns and explain how you'll address them. If you involve them before you start to draw up your telecommuting proposal, they're more likely to help you out down the road if you need it. If you leave them out of the process and then just decide to spring your plan on them one day, you can bet that this lack of regard for their feelings will come back to haunt you.

You might be in the habit of checking with your supervisor to get some feedback or an informal go-ahead before you proceed with a particular task on a project. When you're working from home, this will probably change. Your supervisor won't want you to e-mail every time some little thought pops into your head about some aspect of the project you're working on. So you may have to change your tack: Either save all of your thoughts and great ideas for one time of the day, then blurt out everything at once, or take the initiative and make the decision as to what you should do on your own. Chances are that your boss will approve. After all, asking if you can work from home shows great initiative. You should continue in that vein and make your own decisions about the small things on your own time.

PROFILE OF A TELECOMMUTER: CHARLIE COPELAND

One Friday in January 1992, Charlie Copeland found out that his wife was pregnant with the couple's first child. The next Friday he was laid off from his job at an insurance company he had worked for since December 1982. By the end of that weekend the Copelands decided that Charlie would take some time off and stay home with the baby. He received some severance pay, picked up a consulting job for a few months, and tried to maintain his contacts at the company in the meantime.

The Copelands' son was born in September 1992, and Charlie stayed home full-time until August 1993. For the year that he was caring for his son, he called people he knew at work every few weeks to see if they knew of any positions that were to become available in the near future. One day a former colleague told him of a job opening, but she didn't think he would be interested in it, because it was considered to be a step backward from his previous position, which had been at the management level and involved technical issues. The available job was a frontline tech support position. "I told her that I might be interested if she would let me do it from home," he said. It took awhile to convince the company, but in the end management agreed to let him do the job from home.

First Charlie had to be trained, which took four weeks of part-time on-site work during the summer of 1993. His wife is a teacher, so she had the summer off and could watch their son. Charlie's last day of training took place the day before his wife went back to school, so the timing was perfect. "The next day I started telecommuting and staying home with my son," he said.

Charlie had no illusions about the prospect of effortlessly combining work for the company with childcare. "Watching a kid is a full-time job, and trying to work at home with a baby there is difficult," he says. "The only reason I got away with it was because the type of job I had only required a few hours of time a day. At that point my son was taking two naps during the day for a total of four or five hours, so I would work during those nap times."

He generally worked in two-hour chunks. When Charlie was working at home, his son was his first priority; his job was second in line, sometimes even third. "Even when I was working four or five hours a day, it was hard for me to do that every day," he said. "Basically, I didn't need to, and my workload was such that fifteen hours a week was enough." Unlike a full-time telecommuter, Charlie was paid on an hourly basis, and the workload naturally varied: Some weeks he wouldn't work at all; others he would put in twenty hours. Whenever he had that amount of work, he would do a lot of it after his wife came home from work to take care of the baby. He went into the office each Monday to drop off his timesheet, a fifty-mile round-trip. One of Copeland's coworkers lives only two blocks from his house, and she sometimes delivers paperwork to him in order to save him a trip into the office.

He didn't do any work at all in the office at that time.

But once his son reached twenty-one months of age, in May 1994, he entered day care, and Copeland was able to increase his workload and even start working in the office again, albeit part-time.

His son goes to day care between 8:30 and 9:30, and Charlie picks him up between 3 and 4 in the afternoon, which leaves a pretty good chunk of time to work. However, he admits that the experience of telecommuting full-time while his son was at home spoiled him. "Theoretically, I could spend six and a half hours working, but I don't," says Charlie. "I run errands, do things around the house, and also go into the office more." He tended to work in the office three or four times a week for five or six hours a day, and he'd also work at home for two to five hours on the days he spent at home.

In late 1994 Charlie's wife had another baby, and he reduced his hours once again. He's able to vary his workload in part by covering for employees when they go on vacation in the summer and at other times of year—coincidentally, when his wife happens to be home to watch the children. Moreover, his unit tends to deal with new cases, for which a lot of financial data has to be put into the computer. At his company, he says, there's a very seasonal demand for that.

"When we first developed the idea of my telecommuting, the original thought was that I'd work four or five months a year during the peak season, which was fall and winter, and then I wouldn't work at all," he said. "But the way it worked out, some people left the unit permanently, and vacation schedules came up, and during the summer they gave me as much work as they could." He says he enjoys the flexibility but adds that it's a two-way street. "They'll give me as much flexibility as I want, but I have to get the job done on time," he says. "It's not acceptable for me to say that I didn't call this customer yesterday because

I was working from home and I didn't want a long-distance phone bill."

He says his boss and coworkers help him out a lot, adding that if they didn't cooperate, his arrangement wouldn't work. Besides his neighbor who delivers paperwork to him, other coworkers will check his mailbox every day; if he's expecting something, he'll call them and ask them to watch out for it. For instance, he may be expecting a computer printout that he has to deliver to someone the same day. "I'll call someone in my unit and tell them what the printout is going to look like and ask them to watch for it," he says. "Then, when it comes in, they'll get it and call me, and they'll deliver it to whoever needs it. Sometimes that means walking across the hall and delivering it to someone in a different department, or mailing it out to a client, or sending out computer tapes. It can get complex. The coworker will have to go to the computer center, put a label on an envelope with a return address, and take it down to mailroom with a cover letter, which can mean that they have to take a half-hour out of their day. I do try to do these things ahead of time when I'm in the office, but there have been times when something would become urgent. I've gotten a call at 2 p.m. telling me that a particular tape needs to go out today, when I just got done creating it five minutes ago."

Of the thirteen people on his team, he's the only one who telecommutes, but he says the others pretty much regard him as just another person on the team. They do run into trouble with the team's unit meetings, however, because there will be times that absences due to vacation or illness force the meeting to be canceled at the last minute. When that happens, Copeland says, someone will just walk around the office five minutes before and say the meeting's canceled. He doesn't find out, so he dials into the conference room where it's been scheduled—and takes the consequences.

"One time, our meeting got bumped up into the cafeteria, where there wasn't a phone, because another group needed that room," he says. "I called in looking for the meeting, but the people in the room just picked up the phone and hung up. I called back again and I told them I was looking for my boss, but the person who picked up the phone said she wasn't here and she hung up real fast. I figured I got the wrong number, so I called again. By this time some guy in the room was getting mad, but he finally told me that the meeting got moved. It was a last-minute thing, but no one thought to call me."

He adds that his coworkers do take minutes at the meeting and pass them out later. He gets the basic information, but it can be frustrating because the minutes sometimes don't tell the whole story.

Another problem regarding communication occurred when he first started working from home. Back at the office, he has a workstation with a PC, but not a phone. "In the beginning, people would walk over to talk, see that I wasn't at my desk, and leave a note on my desk. The only way I could get a message from them was if they called or sent e-mail. A couple of days later, when I never answered their note, because I never knew about it, they'd call my boss, and my boss would call me, and I'd tell her that I never got it," he said. "And then she'd have to tell that person that leaving a note on my empty workstation wasn't good enough. I never made a formal statement that I wasn't working in the office anymore, though I did tell some people that I was working from home and if they needed to reach me they needed either to e-mail me or call me. That is a little bit out of the ordinary, and people were kind of resistant to it." But because he's worked at the same company for many years and has been working with the same people, it makes it easier for him to telecommute.

He also has run into problems when dealing with people outside of the company. "They'd call me at home and get my answering machine, and they wouldn't leave a message," he said. "So they'd call my boss and say they got a wrong number because they reached somebody's answering machine. Telecommuting is just a bit unusual so that it throws people off, which can result in some delays in communication." Copeland says he does have turnaround times for his projects, and delays sometimes make it tougher to meet those turnaround times.

When he is working at home, he says, he doesn't usually meet with a lot of distractions. "People don't ordinarily knock on my door during the day very often. People who call me on the phone tend to be someone from work, but occasionally it will be a salesperson. What I don't get is somebody walking by who I haven't seen for awhile to sit down and talk for half an hour, which happens quite frequently at the office. At home I can hide from that kind of distraction a whole lot easier, and it does let me be more productive."

He says that because he works at home, his son doesn't understand that Copeland works. "When my wife goes to work, Jamie stands at the window and waves at my wife," he says. "With me, he runs to the window but never sees me go to work. It's a little bit confusing to him."

Even though Copeland technically works part-time for the insurance company, he still receives some benefits, but his wife, who works full-time, pulls in the bulk of the benefits for the family. Although Charlie has the temperament for working at home, his wife would never be able to do it. "For example, my wife and I hang around on Saturday. But on Sunday she goes stir crazy and has to go out. She wouldn't do well at telecommuting," he says. "But with a young baby, there are times when I don't leave the house for three or four days. I can cope with that, but some people can't.

With any job, you tend to take contact with other people for granted. But if you're telecommuting and you have a baby, that contact pretty much goes away, and you probably won't know how valuable it is until it is taken away. I'm okay if I don't talk with someone on my team for three or four weeks. But the people who spend all day at their jobs talking, they wouldn't do as well.

"It's one of those things that from your coworkers' point of view—working from home, the short days—seems to be real good on the surface," says Copeland. "When I do go to the office to work for a three- or four-hour day, I'll be the last one to get there and the first one to leave. And as I'm getting my coat on to leave, someone may say, 'Boy, I wish I had your job.' And I normally tell them, 'You can: Go talk to my boss, she'll let you. Oh, one more thing: there will be a little change in your paycheck, too.' They always say they don't want it that badly. There's definitely a price I pay for this flexibility. Yes, I've got all the flexibility in the world, but it takes a lot of discipline when there's three loads of laundry, a sinkload of dirty dishes, and a floor that hasn't been cleaned in two weeks. I have to be able to sit down and work for four hours and let all that stuff go."

Though he enjoys the flexibility of his current job, after his kids are old enough to be in school all day Copeland doesn't think that his wife will let him stay home. "It's a real trade-off," he says. "We're trading my time with the kids for money. When they're this young, that's fine. In the future, however, I may go back either to frontline management or consulting."

8

What if It's Not Working?

There are two distinct aspects to telecommuting. The technology that makes it realistic to work at home is one; the other is the human aspect. Even though it's been around awhile, the idea of working somewhere other than the office is still new, and it will take time for people to adjust to it regardless of the industry they're in. People will have to learn about it and develop a certain amount of comfort about it over time.

Each individual person has to be comfortable with telecommuting in his or her own mind; he or she must want to telecommute, even if forced into a mandatory telecommuting arrangement. Those who don't want to work at home will do their best to sabotage the program so they can return to the office, where they're more comfortable working. Therefore, a prospective telecommuter has to be mentally prepared for the idea of working from home and being proactive in order to communicate effectively with people back at the office. If there's a problem, the employee has to be ready to pick up the phone and contact his or her supervisor and/or coworkers.

Indeed, one of the most common complaints telecommuters have in making the adjustment to working at home is the loss of face-to-face contact with people in the office. In fact, in the March 1995, issue of *Home Office Computing,* a magazine directed toward entrepreneurs who work from home as well as telecommuters, 29 percent of the respondents in the annual reader survey said they miss office socializing the most, while 27 percent said they missed having an assistant or secretary to work with. Fifteen percent said the thing they missed most about working from home was feeling they were part of a team.

Seven Ways to Relieve Isolation

1. Get in touch with other telecommuters at your company or at others. Check to see who else in your neighborhood is working from home. Though many of the other people who work from home won't take kindly to being interrupted during the day to participate in what may resemble a kaffeeklatsch, you might want to make informal contact and offer an exchange of support. For instance, you may want to offer to accept your neighbor's express mail packages on the days he or she has to be out of town, and your neighbor may ask you for tips on the best way to get a contract from your company. Don't push it, however, especially if you sense that a particular person is not crazy about the idea of socializing during the workday with other people who work from home. Your best shot is with other telecommuters from your company.

2. Take a break by going on-line. CompuServe has a Working From Home forum where you can find solutions to the problems of isolation and give advice to others who are going through what you've already dealt with. Sometimes these "Dear Abby" sessions can even materialize into fruitful working relationships.

3.   One advantage of telecommuting if you're not required to be in your home office every minute from 9 to 5 is that you don't have to save up all your aggravating errands—such as running to the dry cleaners or taking your dog to the vet—for Saturday, when it seems everyone in the neighborhood has the same thing in mind. You can also look to these errands as a way to alleviate your feelings of isolation. Once you visit the supermarket or dry cleaner during the day for a few weeks in a row, the people who work there will start to recognize you and chat with you.

4.   If you regularly took an exercise class or participated in some activity before or after work or during your lunch hour when you worked in the office, then try to do the same thing when you're working from home. This may be a good way to interact with other telecommuters or home-based entrepreneurs in your neighborhood. Find someone to go for a walk or a swim with at lunchtime.

5.   Set up a network of telecommuters in your industry for an e-mail round robin. Someone poses a question or problem, and everyone in the round robin gets to offer his or her two cents' worth on the subject. After awhile, there are no questions asked, just an ongoing forum of advice and comments. The members of the group can even live hundreds or thousands of miles away from each other.

6.   Call your local chamber of commerce and find out if it has a group of members who are home-based and who meet regularly.

7.   Establish a regular schedule and stick to it. Nothing causes the feeling of isolation to grow more than working at home without a break. People who live by themselves

are especially prone to this pattern. Unless you have regular overtime, leave the office and close the door when 5 o'clock arrives. Then get out of the house and go somewhere where there are other people around.

Many people find it difficult to set the alarm, get up, get dressed, and head for the computer instead of heading to the car for a long commute. For some people it comes naturally. For others, however, it's a big chore. Once they're sitting in front of the computer, however, they forget where they are and are able to concentrate fully on the work before them.

It may be hard to believe, but some people actually decide they don't want to telecommute after all and return to working in the office full-time. Some just aren't able to let go and enjoy the sensation of being untethered from the office; and others may find it difficult to create a routine around working at home; and a number of people just miss the office and the social contact.

Troubleshooting

It's a hard thing to admit that the extensive telecommuting plan you pondered, planned, and worked on for so long isn't working out as you thought it would. Should you keep plodding on and hope that it gets better? Or should you scrap your plans and return to the office, tail between your legs?

You should realize that working from home may be very different from what you expected. If what you're doing doesn't feel quite right, ask yourself if your initial expectations for telecommuting were too high. Most of us have worked on a project that didn't live up to our expectations. In that case, you figure out what went wrong, write it off, and try again.

If you're telecommuting, however, you don't have much

time to waste figuring out what has gone wrong. After all, you're supposed to be working. If your productivity falls off because you're trying to figure out another approach to telecommuting, your boss may decide that you should come back to the office, even though you may still want to give it another shot.

The first thing you have to do is determine where things have gone awry. Ask yourself the following questions:

- ☐ Did you over- or underschedule your time?
- ☐ Did you expect too much?
- ☐ Did it take you awhile to get used to working from home, and now you're hitting your stride, only to find that your boss is cynical about having you continue to telecommute?
- ☐ Did you decide to telecommute based on not your own desires but somebody else's? On what you *thought* you wanted, and not what would truly work for you?
- ☐ Are you working all the time?

If any of your answers to the above questions indicate that you need to revamp your telecommuting plan, then do it. Sometimes people who telecommute get so excited about it that they actually can't stop working. Or perhaps they enjoy the tasks they've assigned to the three days a week they're telecommuting so much that they just muddle through the days they spend in the office and dream of going home.

Telecommuting almost requires that you take a broader look at yourself and recognize both your strengths and shortcomings. If you've been working from home for the wrong reasons, you might have to scrap your entire plan and return to the office to work, even though some people may not like it. For instance, maybe you were the department's telecommuting guinea pig; if you fail at telecommuting, there's a good chance your coworkers' chances are shot as well.

So if you're having trouble, it's important to quickly evaluate what's gone wrong. Then retool and concentrate on what will make telecommuting worth it, or go back to what really works for you—the office.

An Unwelcome Return

Sometimes, your colleagues' resistance toward your telecommuting can be difficult to deal with on the days you do spend working in the office. Some telecommuters discover that other employees' perception of them has changed. Often, disgruntled coworkers will express their displeasure by not inviting telecommuters to key meetings. Or telecommuters may find that they don't get the same kind of information or training opportunities that other employees receive.

What can you do to overcome this hostility in the office? The primary thing is to show your colleagues and supervisors that you intend to stay committed to the company and do the same amount of work you did before, if not more. You'll probably become more efficient in your tasks so that work takes less time, leaving you more time for your family and other interests. And you'll probably also be less stressed, which may actually improve your attitude and outlook toward other employees.

But that won't matter to them. It might just be that your coworkers are incredibly jealous of what you've been able to pull off. The best thing to do is to try to win them over to your side gradually, pointing out instances that show you're as committed as they are even though you don't spend forty hours a week in the office. Suggest that they look into telecommuting as well. Offer to serve as their mentor. Ask them what they would do if they didn't have to commute into the office every day. Bring them through the planning steps that you've taken, and give them time to realize that they can start to telecommute, too. Encourage them to take the chance, even though it's scary, because the rewards can turn out to be much greater than the risks.

What's Really Holding You Back?

If you're still hesitating about telecommuting, ask yourself this question: If all of your excuses to avoid telecommuting were taken away, would you then feel that it was okay to go ahead with it? This question, more than any other, will get you to the real reason why you're not proceeding with your plans. Reasons not to change your life in some way are usually linked up to something else.

Sometimes, people who begin to telecommute but then end up returning to the office full-time a few months later have not dealt with their fears about leaving the office behind, even for a day. Either they believe, deep down, that they don't deserve to telecommute, or they can't fathom how the office will be able to survive without their being physically present. So they intentionally sabotage their telecommuting arrangement, then say later that it was no big deal.

These are the people who need to set a structure, stick to it, and allow themselves some time to adjust to the difference. Men and women who are used to being in the office with someone telling them how to spend each minute of their day will tend to wander around aimlessly if they haven't adequately planned to motivate themselves. They probably won't make it as telecommuters.

PROFILE OF A TELECOMMUTER: LORETTA RISEN

Loretta Risen works for the employee relations board of the City of Los Angeles as a senior clerk typist. She telecommutes about one day a week from her home and has been doing so for about three years. "The city offered it, my boss said yes, and so did I," she said. "I already had a computer at home that I didn't really use, but I brought it in and the office equipped it with the same programs I already used at work. Whenever I have a certain amount of work that can be done on the computer, I bring it home and work on it."

Risen says that because she works in a very small office, with only three full-time staff members, she has to take into consideration who's going to be there when she works at home. At home she's not hooked into the office over the phone lines. She brings a disk home, works on her computer at home, then brings the files back to the office with her the next day and prints them out. Though she lives only about twelve miles from the office, the amount of time it takes her to get there varies. "If I leave my house at 6:30 in the morning, I'll get there at 7. But if I leave the house from 7:30 on, it would take me an hour to get to work."

She says that she gets a lot of work done at home because she doesn't get interrupted by people coming in and telling her what they did on their weekends. "I also don't get the phone calls that aren't for our department from people who are just looking for information. And if I'm not feeling 100 percent that day when I'm staying at home, I don't get somebody else sick," she says. "It's a breather, because I always go in the next morning feeling refreshed."

In order to decide which day she's going to telecommute, Risen looks at the workload at hand. She knows what needs to go out immediately and what can wait a couple of days. "And if I know on Friday that one of the unions is going to give me 100 cases to type up on Monday, then I know I can stay home on Tuesday," she says.

When she's working at home, she calls into the office three times a day: once in the morning, again after lunch, and then at 4 P.M. In addition, her boss telecommutes at least once a week. The other employee in the office does not have a computer at home, but there have been a few assignments she has been able to do at home, according to Risen.

Risen says the best way to anticipate which employees will do well at telecommuting is to look at each person's attitude. "It's all up to the individual," she says. "There are people who will do well, and they'll realize they can get a lot more done at home without the interruptions. Maybe they can't go all the way through to 4 P.M., but they have to realize that they can accomplish a lot more at home than they could at the office. Then there are going to be some people who don't like it, who *have* to be in the office. Both types need to be able to work together and figure out who's going to be able to stay at home and who needs to be in the office."

Risen has an eight-year-old son who was in preschool when she first started telecommuting. She never told him that she occasionally worked at home because "I didn't think that I could get any work done with him under my feet, so I always sent him to school anyway," she says. "But a new mother who has a very young child who sleeps most of the time can definitely do the work at home and telecommute as well."

She admits that there are a lot of managers at the city who are against telecommuting because they can't watch over the person doing the work. "The supervisors have to be retrained in order to realize how much work the person is doing at home," she says. "Now that my boss sees how much work I can do at home, he trusts me. But then, my work is something where you can actually see the product. I'm going to keep telecommuting because I think it's great."

9

What's Next?

The greatest strengths of telecommuting are its inherent flexibility and its ability to adapt easily to new societal and technical trends. Telecommuting may arise at different companies for a number of reasons, but the way that each person involved—telecommuter, supervisor, and coworkers—deals with it determines whether it succeeds or fails. And telecommuting can be combined with other types of flexible work trends such as job sharing, part-time work, and staggered work hours, just to mention a few.

Despite the nay-sayers who exist in the face of any substantive change in society or the work place, people have learned about the advantages of telecommuting and will push it forward so that one day it will be as commonplace as working in an office. Already, telecommuting is being lauded as a big reason why the U.S. work force has increased its productivity.

One of the tools that will be used more and more by telecommuters is videoconferencing. Videoconferencing is boosting productivity among office-bound workers at major corporations. At Hewlett-Packard, for instance, teleconferencing tools have decreased product development by 30 percent. And a spokesperson for American Greetings Corporation reports that it takes less time for decisions to be made on all levels because of videoconferencing. The company attributes this improvement to the fact that more people take part in the meetings, which means that fewer people have to report to their supervisors; most likely, the supervisors have participated in one of the significant videoconferences leading up to the decision.

As with telecommuting, companies that use videoconferencing report an increase in efficiency. Meetings take 20 to 30 percent less time because the participants are more focused; when you're on camera, there's not much room for small talk.

Some employees complain that the increase in videoconferencing has cut down on travel, but the majority of businesspeople who spend anywhere from 20 to 50 percent of their time on the road probably welcome this new technological development as a way to stay put more. Companies also welcome it for the huge amounts of money it shaves off the annual travel budget. And telecommuters like it, because they can be included in important meetings without having to show up at the office.

Telecommuting is likely to grow throughout the rest of the 1990s and beyond, along with other flexible work arrangements that respect the fact that employees have other loyalties than their allegiance to the company. Telecommuting is not going to be right for every employee, but for those who want to take advantage of it, working at home is the first step toward a well-balanced life.

One major development that will come with telecommuting's popularity is the economic rise of rural America, which is always overlooked when new technological developments come around. One of the biggest kept secrets in

America today is the wealth of highly skilled people who live in rural parts of the country. They choose to live there because where they live is more important than what they do for a living, and although small, specialized businesses in need of highly skilled employees do exist in these areas, they exist only on a small scale. With the advent of tele-commuting and remote technologies, rural workers who have previously been underemployed can now work at skilled occupations and therefore bring more money into their communities. If practiced on even a moderate scale, therefore, telecommuting can have far-reaching implications for the well-being of many rural communities across the country.

One problem that may develop if telecommuting becomes an ingrained part of American corporate culture is that suburban sprawl, already a problem in many metro-politan areas, may worsen as fewer people worry about ungodly commutes five days a week. More people will decide to live in rural areas that are outside the suburbs, beyond the point that is thought to be a reasonable commute to the city. Although such growth may bring economic benefits to an area that had been sparsely populated, rapid development can wreak havoc on the infrastructure of an area that is ill-equipped to handle it. In the coming years, the increase of telecommuting will certainly help to shape development in these areas. You should be aware that restrictions and zoning will be par for the course.

The Future of Telecommuting, According to the Experts

"It would be foolhardy to say that telecommuting is widely embraced by corporate America," says consultant Gil Gordon. "There's still a lot of entrenched opposition out there, which I think is due to misinformation and myth. However, there's a growing number of managers who say 'This makes sense, let's try it,' which is a refreshing change in mind-set." Gordon doesn't know whether this new receptiveness has developed because companies are hiring younger people in management or because companies have more experience working with employees who are mobile. "After all," he says, "ten years ago we didn't have people carrying their laptops all over the place and constantly checking their voice mail and e-mail. That was still on the fringe. By and large, office work had to be done in an office. Today people's experience with working in many different locations has grown, and so has their acceptance."

Gordon sees three possible futures for telecommuting, depending on the intelligence of the individual organization. At some companies telecommuting will continue to dribble along as it does today. At other firms it will become more widely accepted, but not quite uniformly used; maybe 3 to 5 percent of all employees will be telecommuting one or two days a week. The third and most likely development is that companies will make telecommuting so much a part of the way they do business that they won't think there's anything special about it. "It doesn't mean that everybody is going to be home five days a week," says Gordon, "but people will be able to work where they work best on that particular day, which is really a natural choice."

In the next five or ten years, Gordon thinks, there will be two dramatic changes that will help to push telecommuting along to greater acceptance. One is that companies will start to rethink their facility plans and office requirements, representing the last break away from the industrial revolution. "We no longer need to give every employee 150 square feet of space just because that's the way we've always done it," says Gordon. The second development will come on the technology side. "I think the real change in technology will not be in hardware but in the software and the telecommunications side," he says. "After all, we've gone as far as we can go for awhile on the computers, unless we find another way of inputting besides our fingers, and computer manufacturers can't make laptops much smaller than they already are." He points to groupware, remote LAN networks, and other software that will help connect one computer—and one person—to another as great opportunities for the future of telecommuting. As more of this software emerges, it's just going to make it that much easier to telecommute, Gordon believes.

But a lot also depends on how well management recognizes the value of telecommuting and learns to work within its always flexible parameters. Managers who work with telecommuters not only learn to manage these employees better but also improve their supervision of employees back at the office. It's difficult to manage in two totally different styles: by presence for in-house employees, and by results with telecommuters. Often, managers will bring their in-house management style in line with the way they deal with their telecommuters, and they are able to view drastic and positive results. In short, managers become better managers overall when they work with telecommuters.

Emily Bassman of Pacific Bell says that within the next few years the work culture will evolve to the point where the term *telecommuting* is not used to denote something different or separate. "People will begin to view it as just another way of getting their work done," she says. "I think that people are going to be so mobile in their jobs that they'll be able to work from wherever they are." But she adds that business will have to continue training managers to manage people who are working remotely. "Companies are going to actually have to provide some training, because it's not necessarily an intuitive thing, and it can be a big barrier sometimes," she says.

Jack Robertson, also of Pacific Bell, agrees with his colleague when she says that telecommuting has nowhere to go but up. "We definitely see it as a growing trend," he says. "One advantage is that once you start a telecommuting program, you're automatically setting up a disaster recovery program as well. That's what happened after the earthquake. Many managers felt uncomfortable with the idea of having their employees telecommute, but they thought that they had to get *some* work out of them as opposed to getting *no* work out of them, so a lot of those management barriers got thrown to the side." Robertson says that Pacific Bell conducted a survey of 1,300 people who started telecommuting after the earthquake. More than a year later, more than 90 percent of them were still telecommuting.

Mike Gorodezky envisions telecommuting as spawning a huge support industry that will grow up around the flexible workplace. "There will be people at telecommunications businesses who specialize in keeping you hooked up with your office," he says. "Videoconferencing will be part of that, too, and as a result, air travel will go way down because people will need to travel a lot less."

He also predicts that office vacancies will rise. "Our company owns an office building. We have two vacant floors, so we could either rent them out or start to spread out into them," he says. "But one has to wonder why we are building these little cubicles for people when they have to work at the end of a phone line and they could easily do it from home."

Staying on the Career Track

One of the biggest obstacles a telecommuter can encounter is a manager who focuses on an employee's attendance instead of his or her output, who bases evaluations on presence rather than effectiveness. In particular, managerial style can affect a telecommuter's chances for a promotion.

"There are many people who get a great sense of power from looking over a room full of people with their heads to their desks, even if they're all doing crossword puzzles," says Susan Herman. "It gives many managers a tremendous sense of power. But what they should really be thinking about is that the only way they're going to get promoted is if the people they're managing are producing more widgets, providing more service to their customers, or whatever. Ultimately, the boss is going to do better and go further if they have people who are helping them to do that." She adds that telecommuting gets high marks in both these areas because employees are happier and feel a sense of control over their lives for the first time ever. "Imagine having happy employees who are producing more," says Herman with wonder. She acknowledges that getting to this mindset requires a definite shift in the mental state of most managers. "It takes some nurturing, some nudging, and some safe harbors of training in order to make that shift take effect," she says.

Jack Robertson, also at Pacific Bell, says falling behind on the career track is what every telecommuter fears. However, telecommuting has really helped his career progress because of his increased output and improved morale. He has been promoted to high levels that he's not sure he would have been able to reach if he wasn't telecommuting. "To me, out of sight, out of mind is an unfounded fear," he says. "You just naturally have to become more organized so that everything tends to take care of itself."

Implementing a Companywide Telecommuting Policy

If you are your company's guinea pig when it comes to telecommuting, the first to spend some or all of your time working away from the office, some of your coworkers will undoubtedly want to investigate telecommuting for themselves. Not only will they ask you about your own experiences, but perhaps your supervisor, the human resources director, or even the president of the company will ask you to help draw up a telecommuting policy for the entire company.

You can use your own experience to advise them, especially since you had to put yourself in the company's shoes earlier in order to ask yourself how working from home would benefit not only you but also the company. Drawing up a telecommuting policy takes the whole thing one step further. Use the following outline as a guide that can help steer your company in the right direction. (If you're still developing your own plans to telecommute and are still working on your proposal and convincing your boss, you can use some of the details here to help fine-tune your own telecommuting arrangement.)

1. Who's going to coordinate a telecommuting program at the company? From what department will this person ideally come? What functions will the coordinator fulfill?

2. The coordinator, the company, and the telecommuter will all need input from the various departments that will be affected when an employee works away from the main office. Will each department have its own representatives? Will they meet regularly, or only when an employee voices a desire to telecommute? What duties will they cover? (See the following checklist.)

_____ Develop policy

_____ Develop telecommuting agreement

_____ Set terms for equipment usage by telecommuters

_____ Set initial goals

_____ Write policy guidelines

_____ Select and evaluate telecommuters

_____ Select and evaluate managers

_____ Select suitable jobs

_____ Promote program

_____ Decide how telecommuters and telemanagers will be trained

_____ Determine if home inspections are necessary

_____ Provide progress reports

_____ Other

Future Technology

The experts like to say that as telecommuting becomes more popular and technology becomes more highly developed, both employees and businesses will get used to the fact that information commutes, rather than people. Future technology utilized by telecommuters will incorporate cellular networks that make it possible to use phones, faxes, and computers without being plugged into a wall jack. Another innovative technological development on the horizon involves portable phone numbers that automatically follow you with the punch of a few buttons on your phone. And as employees—whether telecommuters or not—are beginning to assume more of the responsibility for doing what expensive secretaries used to handle, the hand-held marvels called personal digital computers will become more prominent in the telecommuter's world.

As complex fiber-optic cables are laid throughout the United States and overseas, the ability to telecommute and communicate by both voice and image will be enhanced. For instance, the fiber-optic cables in use in 1994 can process 25,000 calls at once. As the cables become more sensitive and are put into service along heavily used tele-communication routes, they will be able to process 25 million calls at once, or the equivalent of 25,000 television signals.

Another space-age high-tech development involves the assigning of private television stations to an individual in much the same way as a telephone number is assigned to you today. A system called the Bidirectional Unicable Switching System, also known as BUSS, will make it possible to have exclusive videoconferencing no matter where you go. Each person who uses BUSS subscribes to the cable system and will receive the equivalent of a private TV station. Though this technology is still in development, it is quickly moving toward the day when it will become commonplace. Employment analysts believe that the quick development of interactive technological systems like BUSS will only help the United States to stay competitive in the international business world.

Downsizing Your Job

Once you adjust to telecommuting, you may find that you like it so much that you want to do even less of it; that is, you want less work and more of the freedom and extra time you enjoy so much. You may find that your job doesn't quite fit your priorities the way it used to. You've changed, and you may find yourself thinking about quitting your job because your company couldn't possibly be any more flexible.

Don't jump yet. If you're happy with your company, and it has been pleased with your work, you might approach your boss about switching to another job in the same or a different department. Maybe you want less responsibility and/or fewer hours. Though some of your coworkers may look at you in wonder, you should maintain that this is what you want for yourself. It doesn't matter if you're making less money or carry a less prestigious title. If it's possible to create a new position, combining the best of your current job with some new responsibilities, maybe you could pass some of your old duties on to a colleague or assistant. If there's nothing available right away, do what you have to do to get your work done while remaining true to what you ultimately want to do with the company within the context of your new outlook.

PROFILE OF A TELECOMMUTER: DONNA CUNNINGHAM

Donna Cunningham has been working for AT&T Bell Laboratories, based in Murray Hill, New Jersey, since 1980. She's held various positions there. In 1989, when she met the man who would become her husband, she was working as a global media relations manager for the company.

She had assumed that when she married her husband—a Vermonter who was less than enthusiastic about moving to New Jersey—she would have to leave her job. "I told my director that I loved working for Bell Labs, but a six-hour commute wasn't going to work," says Cunningham. "To my surprise, she suggested I take my job with me. I already had a computer that was supplied by the company so I could work at home and read my e-mail on the weekend." When they decided that Cunningham could do her job from 400 miles away, the company also set her up with a videophone, two-line cordless phone, answering machine, fax machine, computer printer, and modem. This equipment allows her to work easily with the department secretary back in the New Jersey office. "If I need to get certain things done, I just fax a note to her," says Cunningham. "When

she finishes it, she just faxes it back to me. We have everything in writing and it's very convenient."

Cunningham says it took no time at all for her to adjust.
"I had been doing so much electronically anyway on the
phone or by e-mail that I don't think many people even realized I was not physically in the New Jersey office. People
realized after awhile that I had moved, because they noticed
that when they returned my call they were calling another
area code." But, she adds, there were people who didn't
know that she had moved until two years later. If a reporter
called Cunningham's New Jersey number, the secretary
would transfer the call to her up in Vermont without a
hitch. "Some people at the Labs still think I'm in New
Jersey," she laughs. "Sometimes they notice that the head-
er on the e-mail or fax is different at the top, and that's
when they'll say something."

To maintain contact, Cunningham travels to New
Jersey once or twice a month, and she still attends conferences around the country, flying out of nearby Burlington,
Vermont. Some of her colleagues also work at home, but
usually only for one or two days a week. "They call me the
ultimate telecommuter," she says. "But essentially, I'm just
a little farther down the hall than I used to be."

One disadvantage of telecommuting is that
Cunningham has to work to keep tabs on new developments in the labs. "It's a little harder for me because I can't
just bump into somebody in the hall," she says. "When I'm
in New Jersey, for a couple of days for a meeting or media
visit, I'll stay an extra day so I can spend time in some of the
labs just so I can keep up on how things look and what's
going on. I like to meet with people in person and find out
what they're doing or meet with a whole department and
let them know I want to hear from them if something
newsworthy happens."

She says that when she started working from home,

telecommuting was nothing radically new at the company. "We've always had people telecommuting informally," she says. "If you had a need, you just did it. Managers feel that if you have something that requires concentration and quiet, and if you don't need to be in a lab, it's often possible to work from home."

Cunningham says she's had an overwhelmingly positive reaction from people, whether they're coworkers or press contacts who call her for information. "Frequently, reporters will call late at night or on weekends, and they apologize for calling, but I've never minded helping them at that time. At AT&T, we include our home phone numbers on all releases and advisories that we send out to the press. The advantage I have is that I already have everything I need to respond right here in my home office," she says. "I can fax or e-mail documents as I'm talking to a reporter. If I were still in New Jersey, I'd have had to go into the office to first get the document and then fax it to the reporter."

Cunningham's advice for people who don't want to commute is to work for a company that supports telecommuting. "It makes a difference to work for a company that cares about its employees," she says. "A company that supports telecommuting clearly trusts and empowers its employees."

It also helps if you have a great office space to work in. Cunningham's husband designed their house—he's an engineer and also has a home office—and he knew they'd both have their offices in the house. He designed the first floor of their three-story house with this in mind: one-fourth of the space is her office, one-fourth is his, and the rest is open space with furniture, a TV, VCR, and a woodstove. Cunningham says it's convenient because whenever she needs to review a videotape for work, she can do it right there next to her office. She likes to work with her "office mate," Coda, a golden retriever, by her side.

Though she's always been comfortable with her job responsibilities, she's not sure a person could just walk into any job and do it from a remote place right off the bat. "For instance, if I have to talk to a reporter and tell him what a particular laboratory looks like, I'd better know what it looks like," she says. "I have to know our scientists, engineers, and executives and be knowledgeable about Bell Labs' research and development work. I'm not sure you could get that information if you were telecommuting full time from the beginning. I don't go to quite as many meetings now, although I conference myself into some of them either with a videophone or a regular phone."

She says the company is not losing any money through her telecommuting; in fact, she says, it's breaking even when it comes to expenses. Back in 1989, when she and her boss made the decision for her to telecommute, they figured out that the overhead for her New Jersey office was about $9,000 a year. "So instead of providing me with an office and lights and heat, we decided that I would use that money to buy airline tickets to fly down to New Jersey," says Cunningham, who, except for her phone bill, pays for the utilities in her home office

"Sometimes I talk to people who say they would like to work this way but their companies won't let them," she says. "To me, that seems shortsighted on the part of the company. They'd retain valued employees they might otherwise lose, have happier and more productive employees, and probably save money besides."

What's the biggest difference between working at home and working in New Jersey? "Here," she says, "a power lunch means taking the dog for a walk."

Further Reading

Atkinson, William. *Working at Home: Is It for You?* Homewood, Illinois: Dow Jones-Irwin. 1985.

Baetz, Mary L. *Planning for People in the Electronic Office.* Toronto: Holt, Rinehart and Winston, 1985.

Becker, Franklin. *The Successful Office: How to Create a Workspace That's Right for You.* Reading, Massachusetts: Addison-Wesley, 1982.

Cross, Thomas B., and Michelle Gouin. *Intelligent Buildings: Strategies for Technology and Architecture.* Homewood, Illinois: Dow Jones-Irwin, 1986.

Cross, Thomas B., and Marjorie Raizman. *Telecommuting: The Future Technology of Work.* Homewood, Illinois: Dow Jones-Irwin, 1986.

———. *Networking: An Electronic Mail Handbook.* Glenview, Illinois: Scott, Foresman, 1986.

Edwards, Paul and Sarah. *Working from Home.* Boston: J. P. Tarcher, 1984.

Fleming, Lis. *The One-Minute Commuter: How to Keep Your Job and Stay at Home Telecommuting.* Davis, California: Lis Fleming, Ltd., 1988.

Gordon, Gil, and Marcia M. Kelly. *Telecommuting: How to Make It Work for You and Your Company.* Englewood Cliffs, New Jersey: Prentice Hall, 1986.

Grandjean, Etienne. *Ergonomics of the Home.* New York: John Wiley & Sons, 1973.

Gray, Mike, Noel Hodson, and Gil Gordon. *Teleworking Explained.* West Sussex, England: John Wiley & Sons, 1993.

Hewes, Jeremy Joan. *Worksteads: Living and Working in the Same Place.* New York: Doubleday/Dolphin, 1981.

Kinsman, Francis. *The Telecommuters.* Chichester, Great Britain: John Wiley & Sons, 1987.

Korte, Werner B., Simon Robinson, and Wolfgang J. Steinle. *Telework: Present Situation and Future Development of a New Form of Work Organization.* Amsterdam: Elsevier Science Publishings, 1988.

Mason, Roy. *Xanadu: The Computerized Home of Tomorrow and How It Can Be Yours Today.* Washington, D.C.: Acropolis Books, 1983.

Midwest Institute for Telecommuting Education. *The MITE Telecommuting Implementation Manual.* Minneapolis: MITE, 1994.

National Academy of Sciences. *Office Workstations in the Home.* Washington, D.C.: National Academy Press, 1985.

Nilles, Jack M. *The Telecommunications-Transportation Trade-Off: Options for Tomorrow.* New York: John Wiley & Sons, 1976.

Olmsted, Barney, and Suzanne Smith. *Creating a Flexible Workplace: How to Select and Manage Alternative Work Options.* New York: AMACOM, 1994.

Ramsower, Reagan Mays. *Telecommuting: The Organizational and Behavioral Effects of Working at Home.* Ann Arbor, Michigan: UMI Research Press, 1985.

Schneider, Jerry B., and Anita M. Francis. *An Assessment of the Potential of Telecommuting as a Work-Trip Reduction Strategy: An Annotated Bibliography.* Chicago: Council of Planning Librarians, 1989.

Short, John, Ederyn Williams, and Bruce Christie. *The Social Psychology of Telecommunications.* New York: John Wiley & Sons, 1976.

Silberstein, Judith, and F. Warren Benton. *Bringing High Tech Home.* New York: John Wiley & Sons, 1985.

Sullivan, Sandra A. *Home Is Where the Office Is.* Flex-It: Southington, Connecticut, 1994.

————. *What You Don't See Is What You Get.* Flex-It: Southington, Connecticut, 1994.

Toffler, Alvin. *The Third Wave.* New York: Bantam Books, 1980.

Wheeler, Michael, and Dana Zackin. *Work-Family Roundtable: Telecommuting.* New York: The Conference Board, 1994.

Newsletters

Telecommuting Review, Gil Gordon & Associates, 10 Donner Court, Monmouth Junction NJ 08852.

Work Times, New Ways to Work, 785 Market Street, Suite 950, San Francisco CA 94102.

Home Office Computing, P.O. Box 53560, Boulder, CO, 80322

Organizations

Association of Part-Time Professionals, Crescent Plaza #216, 7700 Leesburg Pike, Falls Church, VA, 22043, 703-734-7975.

National Association for the Cottage Industry, P.O. Box 14850, Chicago IL, 60614, 312-472-8116.

National Home Office Association, 1828 L Street NW, Washington, DC, 20036, 800-664-6462.

Consultants

Gil Gordon, 10 Donner Court, Monmouth Junction NJ 08852, 908-329-2266 (fax 908-329-2703).

Midwest Institute for Telecommuting Education, 1900 Chicago Avenue, Minneapolis MN 55404-1995, 612-879-5409.

Index